THE GUY-FRIENDLY YA LIBRARY

❀ ❀ ❀ ❀

Serving Male Teens

Rollie James Welch

Libraries Unlimited Professional Guides for Young Adult Librarians Series
C. Allen Nichols and Mary Anne Nichols, Series Editors

LIBRARIES
UNLIMITED
A Member of the Greenwood Publishing Group
Westport, Connecticut • London

Library of Congress Cataloging-in-Publication Data

Welch, Rollie James, 1957–
    The Guy-Friendly YA Library : Serving Male Teens/Rollie James Welch.
        p.   cm.—(Libraries Unlimited professional guides for young adult librarians series,
    ISSN 1532–5571)
        Includes bibliographical references and index.
        ISBN-13: 978–1–59158–270–0 (alk. paper)
        ISBN-10: 1–59158–270–9 (alk. paper)
        1. Young Adults' Libraries—United States.   2. Boys—Books and Reading—United
    States.   3. Libraries and Teenagers—United States.   4. Teenagers—Books and
    Reading—United States.   5. Reading—Sex Differences.   6. Reading Promotion.   I. Title.
    Z718.5.W45   2007
    027.62′6—dc22   2006102882

British Library Cataloguing in Publication Data is available

Library of Congress Catalog Card Number: 2006102882
ISBN: 978–1–59158–270–0
ISSN: 1532–5571

First published in 2007

Libraries Unlimited, 88 Post Road West, Westport, CT 06881
A Member of the Greenwood Publishing Group, Inc.
www.lu.com

Printed in the United States of America

The paper used in this book complies with the
Permanent Paper Standard issued by the National
Information Standards Organization (Z39.48–1984).

10 9 8 7 6 5 4 3 2 1

THE GUY-FRIENDLY YA LIBRARY

Recent titles in Libraries Unlimited Professional Guides for Young Adult Librarians
C. Allen Nichols and Mary Anne Nichols, Series Editors

Library Materials and Services for Teen Girls
Katie O'Dell

Serving Older Teens
Sheila B. Anderson

Thinking Outside the Book: Alternatives for Today's Teen Library Collection
C. Allen Nichols

Serving Homeschooled Teens and Their Parents
Maureen T. Lerch and Janet Welch

Reaching Out to Religious Youth: A Guide to Services, Programs, and Collections
L. Kay Carman

Classic Connections: Turning Teens on to Great Literature
Holly Koelling

Digital Inclusion, Teens, and Your Library: Exploring the Issues and Acting on Them
Lesley S. J. Farmer

Extreme Teens: Library Services to Nontraditional Young Adults
Sheila B. Anderson

A Passion for Print: Promoting Reading and Books to Teens
Kristine Mahood

The Teen-Centered Book Club: Readers into Leaders
Bonnie Kunzel and Constance Hardesty

Teen Programs with Punch: A Month-by-Month Guide
Valerie A. Ott

Serving Young Teens and 'Tweens
Sheila B. Anderson, Editor

This book is dedicated to
Lauren, Ali, and Andy.
We soldier on.

CONTENTS

SERIES FOREWORD

We firmly believe in young adult library services and advocate for teens whenever we can. We are proud of our association with Libraries Unlimited and Greenwood Publishing Group and grateful for their acknowledgment of the need for additional resources for teen-serving librarians. We intend for this series to fill those needs, providing useful and practical handbooks for library staff. Readers will find some theory and philosophical musings, but for the most part, this series will focus on real life library issues with answers and suggestions for front line librarians.

Our passion for young adult librarian services continues to reach new peaks. As we travel to present workshops on the various facets of working with teens in public libraries, we are encouraged by the desire of librarians everywhere to learn what they can do in their libraries to make teens welcome. This is a positive sign because too often libraries choose to ignore this underserved group of patrons. We hope you find this series to be a useful tool in fostering your own enthusiasm for teens.

Mary Anne Nichols
C. Allen Nichols
Series Editors

Introduction

Practically all of today's public libraries, regardless of size or financial situation, have allocated staff hours and money to promote and publicize the library's services to its community. Eager to spread the word about the wonderful services the library offers to each citizen, a library blankets its service area with brochures, public service announcements, and signage detailing library events. Patrons can then browse over dozens of booklists (in both electronic and print form) giving recommendations that may appeal to any group in the community. The latest titles by African-American authors, the top books featuring gay and lesbian characters, the *New York Times* bestseller list, and current Hispanic authors are common examples of promotional material produced by libraries. Despite these commendable efforts to connect with patrons, I have rarely come across booklists or programs that specifically target male patrons.

The immediate question is, Why not? The easy, and perhaps too simplistic, answer is that the vast majority of librarians are women. A survey conducted in 1999 by the American Library Association's Office for Research Statistics informs us that only some 21 percent of public librarians are male. It is not unreasonable to believe that librarians constructing booklists do so based on their personal reading, books they have read, and authors with whose work they are familiar; thus, the majority of book promotion targets other female readers. There is nothing wrong with this technique; in fact, if the reader has the same interests and preferences as the librarian, this approach results in great reader's advisory service. But in most libraries' reader's advisory efforts male reading interests are forgotten. In addition, so much focus has been put on the minorities and women who are discriminated in other arenas that in the society as a whole, males are often not considered as a population with special needs.

Now consider the teen population today. In many professional books emphasizing library service to teens, Patrick Jones has consistently stressed that the percentage of teens in the United States' population is between 23 and 25 percent. Furthermore, he points out that today's teen are potential voters for future library funding, and possibly future employees. Approximately half of those teens are male. With 79 percent of librarians being female, can teen males realistically locate a male role model or even a display promoting "guy books" in most public libraries? Will males receive adequate information or be directed to their field of interest?

As I approach 26 years of service in the library profession, mostly serving teens, I strongly feel that overall as a group, teen males simply do not receive the "welcome" to the library that other groups enjoy. Displays or printed booklists in a young adult area (if there is a teen area in the library) have a small chance of being geared to guys. At best, these lists include books that appeal to both sexes, something along the lines of, "If you like Harry Potter, Try These," types of book promotions. (Incidentally, in this book I address services for boys that very well may also appeal to girls, but my intent is to promote services for teen males.)

Beyond promotion of services and materials to males, there are many libraries that just are not teen male friendly. Perhaps the staff over the years has developed a negative attitude about teen males based on past disruptions and unrealistic expectations of male teen behavior. The most visible displays of this attitude may be the neglect of teen male tastes with emphasis only on children, teen female, or adult materials. A rigid atmosphere suggesting all patrons must display formal etiquette upon entering the building bewilders teen males. These methods of control, whether intentional or not, are something guys can sense immediately. At best they feel uncomfortable. At worst, they may rebel against the staff.

Again the question is why? In their book, *Reading Don't Fix No Chevys*, authors Michael W. Smith and Jeffrey D. Wilhelm state that when referring to young adult males it is easy to exaggerate and generalize, particularly in the wake of the Columbine shootings. They contend that too often boys are surmised to be, ". . . isolated, lonely, prone to violence, oppressed by a 'boy code', addicted to the visual media, and incapable of the sustained attention that reading requires." If your library's employees view teen males in this manner, then your library is actually working against itself as it attempts to connect with its patrons. Throughout this book detailed presentations of this issue are offered.

I have attended dozens of young adult librarian workshops; and the lack of male librarians who serve this age group is amazing. For example, I spoke at the OELMA (Ohio Educational Library Media Association) convention in 2004 on the topic, "Books for Reluctant and Not-So Reluctant Readers," a definite young adult topic and one that speaks directly to connecting with male students or patrons. The room was overflowing with 110 school and public librarians, but as I scanned the crowd, a quick count revealed (including myself) five males in the room. This percentage is not abnormal, almost any young adult librarian workshop numbering over 50 participants has only a single digit number of males in attendance.

With the combination of a low percentage of young adult librarians (and librarians in general) being male and a possible prevailing negative view of teen males within the profession, I think you'll agree that my point about library services to teen males as widely lacking is valid.

But is there a solution? It is impossible for library systems to overnight hire thousands of male young adult librarians to provide more comfortable service for teen males. But it's not impossible to change perceptions and attitudes. By writing this book, I hope that public librarians, administrators, middle management department heads, school librarians, and teachers become more aware of the needs of young adult males and what services they want the library to provide. The needs of these young men vary from community to community, from urban to suburban to rural; but like any public library patron, they enter the building in search of something. As a professional librarian in the twenty-first century, you should become more aware of this segment of the population and ask questions about how they can be better served.

What are the needs of male teens? How can your library provide for these needs through collection development and programming? How can the library staff's attitude be improved in regard to adolescent males?

Set a priority on evaluating your library's customer service, and focus that effort on male teens, the demographic group that has traditionally been ignored by libraries.

As librarians, the dilemma we are facing is that not only are male teens losing interest in books and reading, they are also drifting away from any or all library services. Libraries simply cannot afford to ignore these patrons (and potential voters) during their teen years and hope they return 40 years later to rediscover the library when they enter retirement. Considering the current downtrend of library financing, ask yourself this: can your library realistically afford to alienate these patrons?

If your library is not already doing so, start to explore the issue today. Make a concerted effort to comprehend what attracts males to reading and to the library; and expand your findings into a plan to promote the use of the library by male teens. Are the magical items graphic novels of both Western and manga styles available? Could a wide selection of music, especially hip-hop CDs help attract males? Or could the hook be something more traditional such as updated homework reference tools that the school library cannot afford to purchase? How about all of the above?

After pinpointing what pulls guys to your library, conduct a self-evaluation of your facility to discover if there are hidden obstacles that work against the efforts to bring teens and especially male teens into the library. Does your library have an unwritten policy not to purchase CDs with a parental advisory label? Do selectors believe that graphic novels are too violent, or a lesser form of literature? Has the library been remiss in updating the teen area and displays to what is popular? A teen generation lasts 7 years, and during that time almost everything changes in popularity. What is the hottest trend when a teen is 13 cannot be expected to be popular when he or she is 19. Make sure your library staff is aware of the constant changes in pop culture, music, and especially reading formats for teens, and that they incorporate this into the teen collection.

I have written this book from my own viewpoint, as a young adult librarian serving an ethnically diverse, urban population. However, my background also includes working in a county library system that served a small city as well as suburban and even rural communities. Also, I draw from years of experience as a school librarian in several high schools. From these varied experiences, I have gained insights on how to connect with male teens in different environments and of different ages—insights that I'd like to share with you. This book is primarily meant to assist young adult librarians in the public library setting, but school librarians, library administrators, and library associates that come in contact with teens may also find the contents useful.

I hope that library administrators use this book as a guide to construct a plan for a library staff to improve services for male teens and implement that plan with renewed enthusiasm for this segment of their population. I also hope that this book serves as a resource for librarians just entering the library field and choosing to work with teens as well as veteran staff who are interested in updating their service to teens.

Throughout this book, many generalizations are made. Please keep in mind that there are exceptions to practically every circumstance that is presented. Not all teen males are the same. For example, some teen males want to learn how to knit and may be the only guy attending a library workshop on that craft. The key is to not make assumptions and to treat all teen males as individuals, at the same time providing a consistent welcome to the library.

Chapter 1

THE LIBRARY STAFF VS. GUYS: CAN'T WE JUST GET ALONG?

In a prolonged attempt to shatter the image of librarians as detached, uninvolved, and uncommunicative government employees, library administrations today are taking great strides to improve service to patrons. Book clubs are formed to create community interaction and help patrons keep up on the newest fiction and nonfiction, and dazzling facilities are springing up in many suburban and city environments. Information in a variety of formats can be accessed both at the library and at home. Displays range from local history treasures to what's hot in fiction, and are strategically placed to capture the browser's attention.

All of these techniques are designed with the intent to attract a wide cross section of the public to the library, increase their awareness of library offerings, and give them access to the materials that were purchased for the community by tax dollars. However, service to one specific group repeatedly lags behind services to other groups without any noticeably valid reason as to why. The members of this group, making up approximately 25 percent of a public library's patrons, are the teens visiting the library (Willett 1995).

Presumably, a percentage approaching half of that group is teen males, arguably the most misunderstood subsection of any group of patrons that enters the library. Teenage males are often perceived and labeled as rude, disruptive, uncooperative, and not interested in what the library offers—a generalization too often voiced by library employees. How many of us have heard comments similar to these that appeared in an article in *Men's Health* magazine, "Look at them when they're five and you see God. Look at them when they're ten and you see promise. But look at them when they're fifteen and they're looking at five to ten for felony" (Boyles 1999).

Somewhere, somehow, those cute little boys decked out in clean clothes with their shoes tied and hair neatly combed, hanging tightly to their parent's (or grandparent's) hand, trooping their way to an eagerly anticipated library story time have changed. Within 10 years those boys have grown into young adult males who are now proudly adorned with concert T-shirts, sneakers highlighted with Magic Marker artwork, drooping jeans, hair streaked and gelled into spikes, tattoos, ear- and nose-rings, and sporting a scruffiness that comes with beginning beards. Although their appearance has changed, professional young adult librarians must realize that these young adult patrons are still visiting the public library, because they are searching for something the library offers.

Consider this. Male teens may perceive some differences in the library staff they encounter. Yes, the same employees may still be there, but there's a good chance they have adopted a different attitude about these young men. At age 5, these boys toddling along to story time are greeted with smiles from the majority of employees at the library including circulation staff, security people, and maintenance workers. Ten years later, at age 15, those same patrons, now young adult males, are often met with wariness or even hostility. Does the security worker hold the door open for them? Are they greeted with a smile at the circulation desk as they hand over their library card to be scanned? Is there a dedicated young adult professional who is ready, willing, and able to help them locate what they need; and is that professional friendly and approachable? Or have welcoming smiles been replaced by frowns, scowls, or sighs of exasperation now that this patron has entered his teenage years? Is there a helpful person in sight to whom the young men can turn to for help?

Unfortunately, the answers to these questions must often be answered negatively. No, the door is not open; yes, the smiles have been replaced by frowns and not many libraries hire even the bare minimum staff to help the teen patrons. Upon entering the library, toddlers (and their parents) are often greeted by the children's department staff, a group in which each member has a defined specialty to better enhance the children's library experience. In contrast, too often the young adult position is a job maintained by one professional whose job consists of other duties such as adult reference. Or the young adult services may simply be absorbed by a member of the children's department.

When giving presentations, I generally make a point of surveying the young adult professionals in the audience. The librarians who work in a library where their sole concentration is on teen services are always in the minority; the vast majority of teen librarians perform other tasks. The extent and commitment of young adult services often has a direct relation to the size of the library, often librarians at small libraries wear many hats, and young adult services are tacked on to a job description. One librarian, due to the incredible imbalance of her job, gained my utmost respect. She informed me that her position was split between adult reference and teen services but she was also the department head that produced the monthly work schedule for the circulation desk!

Understaffing and lack of resources are definitely part of the problem. But what else is going on? In his excellent book about connecting with juvenile delinquents, *Bring Them Back Alive*, author Jose M. De Olivares suggests, "But as children mature, they become less enduring. They begin to challenge adults. By the time they are teenagers we really don't want them around" (De Olivares 2004). During their teen years, boys' bodies are changing, sometimes seemingly overnight, into larger people who are awkward, clumsy, strong, aggressive, and loud. These characteristics do not translate well in the stereotypical or traditional library atmosphere. It is quite possible that now the same circulation workers or maintenance people that smiled and commented on how cute these boys were, now view the same library patrons as rude and obnoxious. To borrow a comment I have heard far too often, they think, "Those guys don't need to be here."

Now consider the task confronting young adult librarians. Although his or her job description includes the responsibility to "provide services to teens," automatically the deck is stacked against them. At times it doesn't really matter how many teen novels the librarian can provide summaries for or how creative their displays are, the uphill battle is to overcome the entrenched negative attitudes of the support staff; or worse yet, the administration or other degreed employees.

HOW LIBRARIES UNWITTINGLY ALIENATE TEEN MALES

The largest and most visible asset a library possesses is the building itself. Often it is the appearance of the building that draws patrons to the library. Ideally it should reflect the core values of the community which it serves, and the majority of the population should feel welcome to enter the building. The overall impression conveyed by the architecture can often be stunning, and several professional journals highlight top examples of library facilities.

But each facility has also an interior, and that is an area that can be adjusted to entice patronage to the library. What is the overall atmosphere of your library? What message is being sent by your facility and its furnishings? Is it overly neat and organized to the point of being pristine in all areas? Is the teen area simply an extension of the adult area, reminding teens of entering grandmother's perfectly decorated living room? Or perhaps the teen area is simply a continuation of the children's area, where a teen feels immature and foolish by the style of carpet, undersized furniture, or juvenile color schemes.

To create a balance between an orderly and pristine library environment that welcomes older patrons but alienates teens, you must take steps to designate an area specifically for teens. This space does not necessarily have to be a separate room, but it should be a place away from the children's area and the main adult collection (although with easy access to both areas).

The atmosphere of the teen area should be welcoming to teens, and be unique to their tastes, making it a place that attracts adolescents. Determine what makes a teenager comfortable—as evident in his or her bedroom and other hangouts such as music stores, fast food restaurants, and movie theaters. What makes these the places teens willingly enter on their own? If your library feels more like a museum or a classroom than a popular hangout, you can bet that teens will stay away. How does your library measure up? (In Chapter 8 you'll find details on how to create a teen space that is guy-friendly.)

THINGS VALUED BY DISENFRANCHISED YOUTH

Teens, and especially teen males, seem to have a built-in sensor that detects antagonistic attitudes from adults. Following years of working closely with disenfranchised teenage youth, the Youth Opportunities Unlimited organization of Cleveland has compiled a list of things that are of value to this age group. This list is used as an introduction during presentations at professional workshops.

Although this list stems from working with disenfranchised youth, these values can be applied to teenagers in general and especially teenage boys. The list can also be summarized under the heading of "Gaining Respect."

- Toughness (teens do not want to deal with a pushover)

- Ability to see through deception (deception coming from both peers and adults)

- Unusual way of behaving (disenfranchised teens love professional wrestling)

- Unpredictability (teens like to live "on the edge")

- Total acceptance of youth (acceptance coming from adults)

Characteristics of Disenfranchised Youth Value
Source: Youth Opportunities Unlimited Handout **(December 2004).**

Again, author Jose M. De Olivares perhaps states it best, "Teenagers hate being lied to. They see it as an insult to their intelligence and a threat to their emerging independence" (De Olivares 2004).

If a library staff member, unaware of the value teens place on respect and honesty, proceeds intentionally or unintentionally to alienate these patrons, the library is working against itself. Many libraries that take de-tailed measures to ensure customer service often ignore these principles when dealing with teens, especially teen males. If told to "wait a minute," teens perceive being ignored; if asked to step aside they may feel insulted or disrespected by the adult. Jose M. De Olivares clarifies, "A teenager's personal clock is different from an adult's clock. Adult clocks are depart-mentalized. There is now, later, tomorrow, next week, etc. A teenager's clock only has one setting—now" (De Olivares 2004).

Consider teens' unique assumptions about customer service, and how the library fails to acknowledge these expectations, in the follow-ing not-so-unrealistic situation that could very well occur in a public library.

A local public library is located across the street from a secondary school. The school day has ended and teens burst from the confines of the insti-tution and flock to the library. Inside the library, near the center of the main floor, a group of four teenage boys are crowded around a library table, leaning on the top, arguing over different powers of comic book superheroes. A dozen graphic novels, all that the library owns, are spread out on the table and the boys have pulled from their backpacks their own copies of comic books and graphic novels to reinforce their argument.

On this day, the teen librarian is stationed at the adult reference desk on the opposite side of the room, filling in for an adult services librarian who is on vacation. Sensing a potential noise-in-the-library disruption, the security worker, who has been told to maintain a calm atmosphere, assumes an authoritative stance within 10 feet of the boys' group to keep an eye on things. Pushing a book truck loaded with fiction titles, an adult page sees the pile of graphic novels on the table and says to the young men, "Where did you get those? I don't want to see any of the library's books just happening to find their way into your backpacks!" Feeling that they are being targeted as problems and authority is closing in on them, the boys look at each other and one says as he shrugs his shoulders, "Let's get out of here."

There are several problems here. But before we examine what could be done, consider this possible situation and compare it to the above hypothetical scenario. If the "noisy" patrons were a group of four middle-aged female patrons spreading out design patterns on the table (comparing the library's book sources with samples from the store) for redecorating a kitchen, the security worker and adult page wouldn't acknowledge the situation and would never go as far as to say "I don't want to see any of the library's books just happening to find their way into your purses."

Examining this hypothetical situation, begin with the setting—the boys gathered around a table in the middle of the main library floor. When school lets out, teens have always flocked to the library. Assuming there is no designated teen space that includes study tables, or comfortable chairs near the teen collection, what choice do these boys have? It is amazing that many real life libraries located within as short a distance as 100 yards from secondary schools, do not have a teen area. The teenage boys have selected the library's offerings on their reading passion, are interesting in learning more about their chosen topic, and are sharing books with their peers. These are three goals frequently listed as long-term library objectives. But because they are teenage boys and are adjusting to their bodies and voices, they quite possibly will become loud in the library. Are they disruptive? Certainly. If the noise produced by their argument over superheroes prevents other patrons from concentrating, then, yes these boys are disruptive. Would they be considered disruptive if they were in a teen area, a place removed from the main floor and adult patrons?

And why does the security guard loom over these boys? Teenagers respect toughness. However, at the same time they do not tolerate not being totally accepted. Would a "walk-by" technique by the security person have the same effect for the desired quiet atmosphere? Has the security guard been informed about taking time to talk to teens and the positive effect that communication from adults has on them, or has he only been told to "keep those kids quiet!"

The adult page seems to have undertaken duties other than shelving the books, which is another problem for the entire library beyond the scope of this book. Do the page and the staff member realize that graphic novels are perhaps the hottest reading item in the young adult world today? Has the teen librarian had time to produce a display that promotes graphic novels or a "top-10" graphic novel bookmark that can be placed throughout the library, or is his or her split-time job dominated by expanded duties at the adult service desk? Might the librarian consider asking the teens to help with such a project?

All these questions point to the almost universal customer service problem that confronts public libraries when dealing with teenage boys. Although in this situation the boys did not ask for assistance (and how many adult patrons actually ask for help?) their customer service needs were not effectively met. Believing they were treated with minimal respect, these four patrons of the public library chose to leave the building. Having witnessed many similar situations in public libraries, I know that what often happens after the teens leave is that an employee will say something to the effect of, "I'm glad they're gone." So the library has lost some patrons and since they were only some boys "wasting time," it is often treated as not a big deal. But if this attitude is repeated to the majority of teenage boys who become targeted as problems the minute they walk through the door, then to this group of patrons, the library fails to be used as a community asset.

This unfortunate situation can be corrected by focusing on three areas to improve library services to teens. These three key components of teen service are referred to throughout this book, and they are essential when dealing with teen patrons, particularly teenage males.

KEY COMPONENTS FOR QUALITY SERVICES FOR TEEN MALES

The teen area, and to some extent the entire library, should welcome teens, both male and female, and provide library materials that are up-to-date and meet the teens' interests. Ideally, the area should be large enough to accommodate teens and provide tables for group work, such as discussion and working together on homework. Attention should be given to make the teen area "guy-friendly." However, before we explore the particulars, there are important intangibles besides the physical atmosphere of the teen area that need to be addressed.

Professional Designated as a Teen Librarian

In an ideal situation, this staff member has only teen duties; not a split job between teen services and another task like reference or circulation. Moreover, the teen librarian should have a genuine interest in young adult literature, understand what it is like to be a teenager, and have good rapport with teens, including young adult males. To attract males to the library, the teen librarian should be aware of and provide programs, books, magazines, and music that interest boys.

Library Promotion Materials for Teens

These materials are flyers promoting teen programs, bookmarks that contain annotations centered around a theme, and a teen Web page that provides access to information for teens. Promotional information for teens should equal that for adult or children's services; and it should be distributed throughout the library or library system, not just set in the teen area, or near the designated teen shelves.

Know the Needs of Teens, Especially Teen Males

Making a connection with teen males in the library is a work-in-progress that requires continual effort. Becoming more successful at proactive outreach service, librarians are still searching for help in connecting with teenage boys. At conventions and workshops on the local, state, and national level, schedules increasingly offer workshops and breakout sessions on how to provide quality services to teen males. If you have the opportunity, attend these round table sessions to share and gain information on what works and what doesn't work when dealing with this group of patrons. With recent nationwide budget woes, attending a national conference may not be financially possible, but that doesn't mean you can't find the handouts online. In addition, there are other alternatives if you want to enhance your professional development.

For example, more material is being published on this topic. Although there are several book Web sites that promote books for teen boys, the

Internet provides few Web sites dedicated to only providing material on insights on guys' reading tastes. The http://www.guysread.com and http://www.geocities.com/talestoldtall/BoyMeetsBook.html are two Web sites that are exceptions. The Web site guysread.com is sponsored by Jon Scieszka and geocities.com/talestoldtall/BoyMeetsBook.html is sponsored by Mike Sullivan.

Don't sit back and wait, simply hoping boys will come to your library. Take strides to make your library a place that interests and attracts both teenage boys and girls. The days of merely providing homework help when asked are fading. Seek other young adult librarians in your area, meet with them, pass e-mail and begin to construct a concept of how your library can improve services to teen males. In the Northeast Ohio area, young adult librarians who are employed by libraries that are members of the NEO-RLS (The Northeast Ohio Regional Library System) meet quarterly for several hours during designated afternoons. The purpose of this young adult interest group is to share ideas on ordering, programming and the latest trends that will attract teens to the library. This is just one example of a low-cost opportunity where librarians query colleagues of how to improve and enhance library services to teen males.

Interacting with peers who are in similar situations and are encountering the same problems in teen services is valuable time spent. If there is a similar regional group in your area, encourage your supervisors to build in release time in the weekly schedule for you to attend these meetings and glean information from your peers. The time off the desk is cheaper than attending a national or state convention; and most library administrators are interested in having their teen librarians improve themselves at little or no cost to the library.

After attending a session, share your newly gained knowledge and ideas. By word of mouth or e-mail, share what you have learned with administrators and any other library employee that directly deals with the public (and teen males). These concepts will be further examined in later chapters, but the emphasis should always be on communicating with other library employees. It doesn't make much sense for just the young adult librarian to have the skill to connect with teenage boys and the other staff members continue to alienate these patrons.

THE PROGRAMMING DILEMMA

Along with the current trend of expanding outreach services, there is a growing emphasis on programming. This is a great way to entice teens to the library. However, quality programming takes time and money to develop, and after investing resources, you may not be sure if teens will attend the program. A number of factors affect library program attendance—the school vacation schedule, after-school sponsored activities that conflict time-wise, the weather, or poor publicity can all lead to a poorly attended program.

Over the years, I have witnessed a variety of programs, and some by the program theme that alienate teenage guys. The local Red Cross sponsored a babysitting clinic at my library and was attended by over a dozen teens throughout the 3 days. The problem? The teens were all female. A similar problem would arise from a paint-ball demonstration—it would be almost all males attending. Ideally, library programming would encourage attendance by both teen males and females; but often under the pressure of a "program or die" attitude by an administration, young adult librarians form programs around topics they like or know. And since most librarians are female, programming for guys regularly falls short. Programs designed for only one of the sexes are fine, as long as over time a balance is achieved and the guys get equal consideration. It is unrealistic to hold a make-it, take-it type of craft program (one possibly designed for ages younger than teens) and expect guys to attend. Most craft programs just do not excite teenage males.

But what types of things do appeal to boys? More details on programming can be found later in Chapter 6, but the main thing you should remember is to consider the needs and interests of the entire teen population. Don't fall into the trap of creating a program around what you know rather than what would attract teens to the library. The teen male interest may vary from community to community, but programs listed below, in my experiences, have drawn a good balance between males and females attending.

Halloween costume party (including a theater make-up expert creating realistic-looking bruises and wounds)	Fencing Demonstration
	Monopoly Tournament
Cartooning demonstration (with an evaluation of individual teen work)	Video Game Challenges
	Stock Car Demonstration
Anime Film Festival	
	Limousine preview (to see the inside of a limo before prom)
Hip-Hop Music History	

Teen Programs That Attract Both Males and Females

ESTABLISHING A POSITIVE YOUNG ADULT PRESENCE IN THE LIBRARY

As stated earlier, in many libraries the young adult staff position is a split job, and serving teens is not really a primary focus of the whole library atmosphere. Teen areas are often simply a corner of shelves containing books that are in-between the reading levels of adults and children. There are several progressive libraries that have committed much of that library's resources to the young adult patrons, and these libraries with fabulous teen services should be congratulated, and emulated. One of the first challenges you have as a young adult librarian is establishing a positive teen presence that both the public and the library staff can recognize.

Libraries have traditionally produced a huge amount of promotional print material, and this remains a very good way to also promote teen services. Annotated bookmarks are easily produced and they are doubly effective if they promote books that appeal to guys. Examples of subjects separate from the basic fiction genres that can be formed into annotated lists that will catch a teen male's eye are: "How to Draw Manga," "Dirt bikes," "Four-Wheeling," "NASCAR," "Professional Wrestling," "The History of Hip-Hop," and "The Military" (Special Forces books are a good hook for guys). Achieve a blend in the promotion.

A list of "Hilarious Books for Teens" may include Louise Rennison's adventures of Georgia Nicholson, but should also include Jonah Black's *The Black Book* series for guy interest. Remember, any booklist can also be adapted into a display. But to promote these types of guy books to the library staff, make sure bookmarks are produced in a large enough quantity that they can be placed throughout the library, including at the circulation desk. A display promoting teenage guy books can even be placed on a table near the entrance to the library. Near the beginning of the deer-hunting season (which is very popular with teenage buys in some areas of the country) I made a display of deer-hunting books and positioned it just inside the main entrance of the library. The books constantly had to be replaced, as most of the books were checked out by both teens and adults. If I had put this display only in the teen area, the circulation would likely have been much less. Many adult patrons mentioned that they did not know the library had those hunting book titles. I'm not suggesting that you just start moving tables and setting up displays. Due to the territorial nature of many libraries, this would likely do more harm than good. Find out who in the library has the final say on promotion (this will vary from library to library), and present the need for young adult promotion to that person.

For several years, I have produced a teen newsletter that promotes programs and gives thematic reading suggestions. The newsletter, even if targeted at teens only, is a promotional tool that should not just be set out in the teen area, but should be visible in all traffic areas of the library. I have seen many parents pick them up to take home for their teens. The circulation desk is a great place to set out a teen newsletter. It is the area where most of the library's promotional material is located, and it makes sense that a teen document be distributed in that area.

Other types of promotion can be accomplished through the electronic media. Some libraries have access to local radio and television stations and promote teen programs over the airwaves. Of course, whether you can do this depends on the size of your library and community. Often a smaller community has easier access to this type of media than a large metropolitan library system. When I worked as a librarian in a mid-sized system, the local paper was generous enough to set aside space in the Sunday edition for short book reviews. I write annotations and it surprised me how many adults and teens read them and came to the library looking for those books.

My next step was to include those annotations on the library's teen Web page. A teen Web page is a tool that your library can use to effectively communicate with teens, and it is a great way to appeal to teenage males who are interested in technology. You'll learn more about Web pages and how to use them to attract male teens in Chapter 8.

Displays, teen Web pages, and annotated bookmarks that have guy appeal are all great ways to promote teen services, but the young adult librarian should strive to promote these services throughout the system, not just limit the information to the teen area. The more aware the staff and administration is of the effort to include males in teen services, the more smoothly things can be accomplished when males do enter the library in search of items that interest them.

THE ADULT REFERENCE DESK AND HOMEWORK HELP

One of the obstacles to convincing teenage males to enter the library and use its resources can often be witnessed when guys ask for homework help at the adult reference desk. Nothing alienates a teenage guy from the library more than if he feels he is being ridiculed by an adult. A goal common to all libraries should be to treat teens in the same manner as other patrons, especially if they require assistance. When a teen approaches the reference desk and asks how to obtain sources or needs help locating a specific title or section of the library, that is not the time for the reference librarian to morph into critical teacher or parent mode. This is no time to chastise teens about stretching the deadlines of their papers.

Libraries spend thousands of dollars on electronic resources to speed up the research process and many teens know this, so perhaps it makes sense that they put off their assignments until the last minute. Long gone are the days of constructing a stack of 3 × 5 index cards to take notes and cite sources. Most online databases offer an e-mail feature where the user can send the full text article to his home computer. Don't make the mistake of clinging to "you should have come to the library earlier and I would have been better able to assist you." It is your task to help locate the requested information, even if it is the last minute, something the teens of the twenty-first century are very skilled at accomplishing.

On the other hand, never leap to correct any error the teens have made. Put yourself in the guys' place, and imagine how it would feel if a librarian belittled you, after approaching the adult desk to ask, "Is there any information on the writer George Eliot and did he write anything good?" If the librarian responds with a statement such as, "If you don't know who the author was, how can you expect to find any information?" I can attest that the above situation actually occurred; and the young man walked away, to search the stacks without the aid of a call number, seemingly hoping the information would fall off the shelves into his hands.

It is impossible for a young adult librarian to always step in front of other co-workers to ensure teen patrons are treated with respect. However, one thing that you can do is inform co-workers of potential homework or school research assignments in advance. Most libraries have a "Homework Alert" sheet either on file or posted on the Web. In my experience, those do not work well. I have had better success over time telling teachers (who seem to hate filling out one more form), to simply call me and I would pass on the information to the rest of the reference staff. Of course it takes some time to establish a connection with the school librarian or teacher; and if your library serves several school districts, it can be quite a task. However, being aware of the assignment ahead of time can alleviate the pressure some librarians feel when helping teens, especially teenage boys.

In the end, it all comes down to attitude. The library can have the correct print resources, the databases, and access to the Internet, but if teens feel that when they need help, there is no help to be found, then they will seek information elsewhere, usually by browsing the Internet at home.

SELLING TEEN SERVICES TO THE ADMINISTRATION

One of the toughest tasks to accomplish in improving your services is to make the library administration aware of and the importance of teen services. In some instances, the extent of an administrator's involvement is to hire the young adult librarian, and simply let he or she "create their own niche" in the library. Quality teen services are based on being fresh and up-to-date, which translates into spending money, an area where library administrators demand justification. Circulation figures for young adult materials are usually lower than both the children's department and adult services statistics. So, if your funding is based only on circulation statistics, then young adult will be "last funded, first cut" during budget meetings.

Your goal is to make the administration aware of what is going on in the teen world. Learn ways to promote or advertise what you are doing. If the local newspaper has space for book reviews, write reviews and include guy books! Again, make sure the library is thoroughly blanketed with promotional literature about teen services. A teen Web page will attract boys (and girls) to the library; but a printed newsletter that contains similar information can be passed around by administrators at board meetings. Many directors solicit their staff for updates on what is going on in the library, so the board report reflects a progressive and thriving library. Make sure teen services are mentioned in such reports. If statistics must be included, add to the total statistics how many males attended a teen program. Most library people are aware of the difficulty to attract boys to the library and this is a good and simple way to inform the top levels of the young adult service efforts.

The libraries where I have been a young adult librarian also employed a public relations professional. If this is the case at your library, get to know this person! A simple photograph of teens (including teen boys) appearing in the paper and enjoying themselves at a library function will make the administration take notice more than any booktalk or library display. Depending on the time of year and whether the board is discussing finances, it may or may not be easy for you to attend a board meeting. If the administration levels are too layered to break through, try submitting a written summary of teen services and include some accomplishments that featured males.

Today, many young adult librarians are pursuing the formation of teen advisory boards. This is high profile promotion. Include teen males on your teen advisory board if you can. In Chapter 6, teen advisory boards are discussed in more depth and some tips on how to make these groups guy friendly are included. When planning a teen advisory board meeting, always question, are the goals of that meeting's agenda going to bring guys to the meeting or chase them away?

Library administrators love library connections to schools. Be willing to go the extra mile and establish a connection with schools—remember that is where the teens are! The more you visit the school, the more comfortable guys will be with what you are presenting. (In Chapter 7 you'll find suggestions of how to conduct a school visit and what makes guys sit up and take notice during a booktalk.)

Once a firm connection is made with a school or schools, think about forming or sitting in on a young adult professionals' book discussion group that involves teachers, school librarians, and public librarians. During these talks, young adult librarians can learn about the challenges of encouraging teens, both male and female, to read outside of the curriculum. These opinions come straight from the on-the-frontlines-educators' point of view. Make sure (by a written summary that can be simply e-mailed to them) all levels of the administration are aware of this discussion group, and the school/library connection they form.

Of course, there is no one sure way to sway your administration to become pro-teen. I am constantly surprised by the many libraries who are "just beginning" to implement teen services. You may hear, "This is something we've never done before!" Keep in mind that it takes time, a consistent effort, and you must produce results. Take care to accurately plan any teen service function and promote it. In selling teen services to your library administration, be sure to distribute any follow-up you can provide. Construct a document, it doesn't have to be "official," but it should summarize the program in detail. Include the purpose of the event. Was it something teens asked for? Was it in conjunction with Teen Read Week or National Library Week? Did it have a connection to a school or other agency that deals with teens?

Include any promotional flyer that was connected to the program. A good suggestion that falls under the heading "nothing ventured, nothing gained" is to include in the summary what other publicity would have helped sell the program. Try to research cost of an announcement on cable TV or radio. Could a newspaper ad be taken out? There are ways to promote, but often they are not accepted by the administration. They may want to know how many people will attend your program before investing money into promoting it.

Numbers are what many administrators want to see on reports. Pay attention to the details. Include the cost of the program, how many teens

attended, and include a break down of females and males who partici-
pated. To lay the groundwork for acceptance of future programs, make
sure you thank everyone who helped. No library employee wants to feel
that they are not recognized for their efforts. The evaluation should be
sent to all administrators in your library. This may vary on the size of your
library or library system. And don't forget the Friends of the Library or
your Board of Trustees. Often they wish to help but as just you may not
know how to cut through layers of bureaucracy to the top, they do not
know how to connect down to you.

In many ways the bigger challenge of accomplishing teen services lies
within educating the staff and administration of what the teen needs from
that library are all about. Evaluate your staff and discover if teens are
treated differently from other patrons and are the teen guys treated different from the teen girls? Unfortunately, if this problem permeates throughout the library, it takes a tremendous effort to change the attitudes. But it is
worth the effort. Nothing beats the feeling to have a guy in a leather jacket
come up to you and say, "Hey, thanks for helping me on that George
Eliot thing; the teacher liked what I turned in!" And hearing teens ask,
"When is the library going to do this again?" can make the enormous
effort worthwhile.

REFERENCES

Boyles, Dennis. "Teenage Boys!" *Men's Health* (October 1999): 137.
De Olivares, Jose M. *Bring Them Back Alive: Helping Teens Get Out and Stay Out of
      Trouble*. Lanham, MD: Taylor Trade, 2004.
Willet, Holly G. *Public Library Youth Services: A Public Policy Approach*. Norwood,
      NJ: Ablex, 1995.

Chapter 2

UNDERSTANDING TEEN MALES

Perhaps one day in your career as a young adult librarian, you will find yourself surrounded by a group of teen guys. Fear not! It's normal for these young men to travel in groups, usually gathering together by age. One day the group of guys hanging out at the library might be younger, perhaps 13 or 14. Another day, the pack may be older and range from ages 16 through 18. In my experience, younger guys rarely mix with the older boys, and the most likely scenario is that a group of boys is comprised of males approximately the same age. However, they are all interested in visiting the teen area for reasons that may or may not be clear. Whatever their age, you quite possibly may find yourself amazed at these unique library patrons and their actions.

As a professional, you may find yourself wanting desperately to assist these guys and make their library visit a productive and satisfying one for both yourself and the teens. However, there is a possibility your well-intended librarian efforts will get sidetracked by the boys' behavior, which may include actions completely different from any other patron group.

For example, the boys may make weird noises with their mouths (something that has a communication pattern of its own) or they may be loud and animated in their movements as they rapidly move throughout the library. Younger teen guys often do a curious I-want-to-run-but-know-I-should-walk quick steps when they think the librarian is not looking. On the other hand, one day the boys may be silent and sullen, slouching in chairs. And for no apparent reason, it is not unheard of a guy suddenly lashing out and smacking another boy next to him. Of course their answer when confronted by an adult is generally, "We're just messin' around!"

So it is a safe bet that the teenage boys will be different—not worse or better, just different—than other library patrons. Also, remember that teen boys are both emotionally and physically different from teen girls. In a profession mostly comprised of females, these differences unique to teen boys may be viewed as "weird" or "rude." Many young adult librarians have heard the dreaded phrase from co-workers, "Your teen guys are acting up again." Note the word "your." Many members of library staffs are eager to shun all responsibility of teen patrons (and their behaviors) to the teen librarian. I have never heard a staff member tell an adult reference librarian, "Your patrons are talking too loud." When dealing with adults, the staff usually combines efforts to serve and process adult patrons' needs. Your goal, as a young adult librarian, should be to achieve an atmosphere where the teens are not looked upon as a menace and where all staff is willing and able to effectively assist the teens.

This could be the toughest challenge for all young adult librarians. Before providing quality service to teen males, you must examine what makes them tick—both physically and emotionally. Once you have a working concept of what these guys are all about, then programming, book selection and all aspects of young adult librarianship can be adapted accordingly to enhance the boys' visit to the library.

PHYSICAL DEVELOPMENT OF TEEN MALES

Different opinions have been offered as to what age is the exact beginning of the young adult years. One theory suggests that young adulthood begins at age 12. Another school of thought is that it begins at age 13. This biological debate is inconsequential and beyond the scope of this chapter or book. However, note that in either age mentioned, the beginning of the young adult years starts during the middle school years. This is the age where the young men leave the confines of a library's children's room and begin to assert themselves in the teen area and other parts of the library.

This is also the approximate time puberty begins. It is fairly common knowledge that there is no set schedule for when puberty happens. It may begin for some boys at age 10 and for others it is delayed until age 15. In either case, this is a time of great change for a young man's body. He becomes taller. Facial and body hair emerge. His hips and shoulders begin to develop, becoming broader. And of course, the sexual organs develop. What is amazing—and possibly confusing—is that these basic changes can happen in any order. Facial hair may develop before the boy begins to get taller. Or, a teenage boy can be muscular and tall, but totally lack facial hair. To compound the confusion, the amount of time for puberty to begin and end varies from boy to boy.

These are the visible changes. However, there are also changes taking place inside a young man's body. He is beginning to attempt to define who he is as a person, and is taking his first steps to become a man. There is a struggle for identity during this time, and at the onset of puberty, boys may say to themselves, "Oh wow, I'm not ready for this!"

What do these large changes, both physically and emotionally, mean for adults—such as librarians or teachers—who work with teen males of this age? Although the age of puberty is a challenge for the teen male, it is perhaps a greater challenge for adults who work in an environment that includes them.

Every year, boys going through the initial stages of puberty begin the school year, entering a middle school grade, most likely either sixth, seventh, or eighth grade. There they find themselves among other boys also going through similar physical changes. Mentally comparing themselves to their friends, they notice that each is changing, but at different rates. In any of these grades there are boys of widely varying heights. Some boys may be the same height they were in fourth grade and others have undergone a tremendous growth spurt that has them towering over their friends at over 6 feet in height. Some boys gain up to 5 inches in height in less than one year. This is a tremendous change to undergo in a single school grade, and the body needs time to adjust to this burst of height. In boys this developmental stage is characterized by fumbling with objects, tripping over nothing or banging heads, knees, or elbows on surfaces such as desks or doorways that a year ago used to be easy to avoid.

Some guys have sideburns and the beginnings of beards while other guys the same age retain the soft baby face of a much younger child. Some guys' faces have begun to thin and they have lost the round, pudgy face look and are on their way to looking older than age 13 or 14.

Muscles begin to burst forth. It is not unusual in an eighth grade class to see guys with "pecs," "guns," and "six-packs," who at first glance seem to at least a sophomore in age. Other guys may look like younger brothers to these muscular boys but are actually the same age or possibly even older.

Listen to their voices and you might hear a deep tone that resonates throughout the room. Or, you might hear a high-pitched squeaky chirp that is practically the opposite of another guy's deep voice. These two boys could be the same age. You, as a young adult librarian, should recognize that these are boys entering the teen area of your library with like service needs even though their outward appearances vary greatly. They are no longer children, nor are they yet men. They are all entering young adulthood, just at different physical rates.

PHYSICAL DEVELOPMENT, TEEN MALES, AND THEIR BEHAVIOR

Because of these large and dramatic physical changes in their bodies, during puberty, teen males change their behavior. Often this behavior is a direct result of what is happening to their bodies. Simply put, they are now bigger, and seem to be hopelessly awkward and clumsy. Boys often cover up this clumsy stage by initiating lots of physical contact. You may see boys pushing, punching, shoving, flicking other guys' ears, or snatching someone else's "stuff." In a library (or classroom) setting, it is not unusual to see a guy get up from his chair, walk to a printer or bookshelf, and on his journey he passes by a male friend. There probably are no statistics on this, but I can assure you that more often than not, the guy walking smacks his sitting friend on the head. They are quite slick about this. It happens so quickly, you as an adult may miss it completely, and only hear the seated guy yell, "Ow! What was that for?"

If the staff at your library does not comprehend this teen male behavior, this quick exchange may escalate into conflict between the staff and teens. Too often, this type of aggressive behavior accompanied with physical contact results in the teen male being told to leave the library. You may hear them plead their case by exclaiming, "We were just playing!"

In their minds, they are. However, your co-workers may deplore how the guys act. You may find yourself the target of complaints and forced to defend or criticize the boys. Your workmate might grumble, "I just don't understand how they can be that loud! What are you going to do about it?" This is a fragile moment and a potential lose-lose situation for you as a teen librarian. Do not let yourself be baited into an argument about appropriate teen behavior; but at the same time, do not blindly defend behavior that is totally disruptive. For now, let's take a closer look at these changing young men.

As their bodies have grown at a rapid rate, the boys also are becoming accustomed to changes in their voices. They sometimes yell without realizing they are yelling. Perhaps they associate whispering or low talking as being feminine and weak. For whatever reason, they simply find it very difficult to speak in soft tones. And not only are they loud, the words are often of the "trash talk" variety where they are trying to show up their friends. This is not the prelude to a fight, but simply a way in which boys demonstrate camaraderie.

Besides not fitting into their bodies and adjusting to a new height, the awkward stage shows in boys in other ways. Their facial features may not be symmetrical. One guy's nose might appear to be huge for his face. Or perhaps, another boy's ears stick way out. Their friends, also going through changes, recognize unusual appearances and, perhaps thankful that it has not happened to them, tend to mock any abnormal characteristic. The insulted guy feels he only has two options: fight or laugh. Thus, boys can be heard downgrading themselves with phrases such as, "I'm such a dork" or "What an idiot I am!" If a teen male finds it impossible to laugh at himself, the scene may escalate into a physical confrontation involving a punch or shove, often with a friend with whom he hangs out with every day. This boy behavior, while not unusual, does not fit well into most library atmospheres. An inflexible traditional model of library decorum has no room for this behavior and the teen males may find themselves being kicked out, no longer welcome in the building.

All well and good, you may say, but what is a young adult librarian to do? Will teenage boys accept the structure that is already in place in most libraries? Or will they come with their own concepts of what is acceptable? Is there a happy medium? The answer to all three questions is yes. Confusing? Let's examine the three situations brought up by these basic questions.

LIBRARY STRUCTURE AND TEEN MALES

Unfortunately, you cannot teleport yourself to enter the mind of a teen male nor can adults become invisible and listen in on teen conversations outside the library. If either trick were possible, perhaps a clearer understanding of teen boys and how they view the library would emerge. Although it is possible they are planning mayhem, I do not believe that guys form a game plan of disruption each time they decide to visit the library.

They don't script their actions for the time they are inside the building, but they do instantly react to any authority presence that they view as unfair or inhibiting. As a savvy librarian, you need to learn how to uphold the basic library behavior expectations while balancing a welcoming atmosphere to teens, especially teen males. How can this be accomplished?

First, familiarize yourself with the documented code of conduct for the library. Sounds simple? This document should be on file in all departments of the library and generally it addresses most behaviors. However, it is very possible the document is filed away so deep nobody seems to remember where it is housed. Unfortunately, in my experience, the wording on the document is often in generalizations and is open to widely varying interpretations. Employees may decide there are no gray areas and enforce rules by springing discipline on an unsuspecting teen who has no idea of the library policy and expectations. Other employees may cut the guys some slack and not stress over borderline violations. The danger here is that the young men may not be able to change their behavior when the help desk shift changes from a "good cop" to a "bad cop."

As a young adult librarian, you may feel you have done an excellent job of welcoming, bonding, and providing a positive library experience for teens, only to find out a complaint has been filed to the administration about the bad behavior of those same teens. The complaint may cite rude or unacceptable behavior. This is where the code of conduct becomes invaluable. You can effectively defend the teens' behavior if you know they did not violate any conduct rules. Don't think this cannot happen; it does. The situation is doubly discouraging when complaints about teens originate not from other patrons, but from your co-workers. Many teens have told me they appreciate me at the help desk, and that my co-workers "rag on them too much." Your co-workers, who feel uncomfortable around teens, may label you as too much of a friend to teens. In their mind, that makes you one of them in their perceived battle of "us versus them."

If your library does not have a written code of conduct in place, strongly suggest that a committee or task force be formed to formulate such a document, and volunteer to be involved. The reality is this: many patron behavior issues that are agenda items at administration discussions originate from teens being in the library.

Becoming familiar with the concepts presented in this code of conduct document will give you an idea of "where the line is drawn" for acceptable and unacceptable behaviors for all patrons. This document can also provide you as a front line service librarian necessary back up from the administration if a serious confrontation should arise.

So, you have familiarized yourself with the rules of the library. How do you make teens aware of what is and is not acceptable as behavior? Communicate the structure's outline in a nonthreatening way. Talk to the teens in a nonthreatening tone. Don't become a sergeant-at-arms and recite the list of rules and tell them what items they have violated. Include yourself in the statement, hinting that "we're working together on this fellas." For example, use the sentence, "Let's get settled here" rather than, "Hey, you! Settle down!" To teen guys, there is a huge difference in those two statements.

Learn the names of teens, at least the names of those who are regulars. Or greet them and ask them their name as they enter your work area. One caution here is not to try to be too cool. Nothing sets males teens on edge than to have an authority figure use outdated slang. A simple, "How ya doin' today?" works just fine.

Other methods of communicating expected library behavior include having a discussion of the conduct code as an agenda item at a teen advisory board meeting. Perhaps you need to have an adjusted code of conduct in place for the designated teen area that is worded in a more teen-friendly fashion. In all these situations of communicating with teen males, the first step is to not approach them in a manner that they will view as overly authoritative or threatening.

TEENAGE BOYS AND GIRLS TOGETHER IN THE LIBRARY

Any discussion about understanding teenage boys must also include dialogue about their actions when grouped with teenage girls. Rare is the public or school library that allows access only to one sex at a time, and the majority of library use by teens will feature mixed sexes. A significant number of my co-workers insist that this mix of sexes is the catalyst for all disruptive teen behavior. The reality is many libraries are adopted as the meeting place for teens, especially younger teens without driver's licenses. One day, you may find yourself in this situation. The guys are online surfing the Web without any problems. Other young men may be reading any variety of materials available. Suddenly, girls enter the teen area. Of course the opposite scenario can occur—that is the teen area is being utilized by girls and guys come in contact with the girls. In either case, you may see a complete change of behavior. Why?

At this age while boys' bodies are changing, so are their feelings sexually. Inside they recognize the girls are different from them and are now considering them sexually. Teens may not be able to tell adults what is going on inside them, but we all know that boys and girls together in a public setting creates a very different situation. The boys want to interact with the girls, but just do not know how to go about it.

In preparation of writing this chapter, I spoke to several teachers and librarians who have worked on the "front lines" for decades. I asked them their thoughts on how boys behave, not as a one-on-one with girls, but how boys behave in a group near girls. Their comments uniformly fell into three behavior characteristics when teen boys and girls are grouped together. What follows is a composite of how boys behave during adolescence when they find themselves near girls.

Overwhelmingly I was told that boys want first and foremost to be noticed and seek any way for that to happen. They are often aggressive in drawing attention to themselves when near girls, but just don't know how to do that appropriately. They may burp, pick their noses, make rude sounds, or blurt out something that is loud and completely off topic. At times, they will do a broad physical stunt such as tripping on purpose, or lift a chair or table just to show their emerging strength. You can easily see how these behaviors may not dovetail into a library's code of conduct document.

A second characteristic mentioned by my teacher and librarians friends when boys are grouped with girls is an excessive amount of posturing. Boys will stick out their chests and actually strut doing simple tasks such as tossing a piece of paper in the wastebasket. My friends also tell me of boys suddenly deciding to wear too-tight shirts to show off arm and shoulder muscles.

I was informed that while boys are in mid-posture, this is a delicate moment in time for them. Choose carefully your words if you wish to correct any disruptive behavior. If a teenage boy feels his actions have gained the attention of a girl, at this time he will not back down from adult authority. In some ways, boys seem to feel a mini-rebellion is a sure way to impress the girls. Have I mentioned that patience is a good trait to have as a young adult librarian? Here is a perfect example of when to "count to ten" when addressing a guy's behavior. Too often, librarians do not understand what is happening and quickly decide the only way to maintain the library's calm atmosphere is to remove the boy who is "talking back."

The third category about teen guys and girls together is that any reaction to anything tends to be over-the-top. If a joke is told, the laughter will be loud and long and might just turn into a competition to see who laughs the longest, loudest, or weirdest. You may witness a single joke turn into an improv to confirm session of "your mama" jokes as the boys try to outdo each other. The girls finally saying "shut up" may or may not slow down this train-wreck of behavior. This is a good opportunity for you as a librarian to use the calming statements that establish you as the catalyst for the behavior change. Try to phrase the request in a neutral way such as, "Let's get back to library stuff here."

The good news? This awkward stage of large motor movements, borderline rude behavior, and showing off for the girls gets under control as the teen males mature. Allow me to describe a previous experience of about 5 years ago with my teen advisory board. I had a new group of teen advisory board members consisting of eight teens, a mix of three boys and five girls, who signed up as freshmen to be part of the board. They came from different schools and were all good students and seemed to be quality individuals. Early on, the boys sat as far away as possible from the girls and I had to draw comments out of them. The boys quickly fell into the "over-the-top" actions. They ate too fast, dropped food, and just seemed to be too big for the chairs in the room. They laughed loudest and longest over any statement trying to annoy the girls. The girls seemed to be much more receptive to library topics and discussions about books and potential programming ideas, but the boys wanted to talk about horror movies and video games. They were great impersonators and imitated sounds bites from movies they had seen and games they had played. Not that horror movies and video games are bad things, but they became very animated and loud, actions that distracted from running a productive advisory board session.

We made it through the initial awkwardness, and the boys stayed with the advisory board for 4 years. I was so pleased to see all that the boys' inappropriate behavior disappeared. Eventually the guys mixed in with the girls, talked about mutual interests such as SAT tests, marching band competitions, and school theater productions. They all became e-mail buddies and progressed on to college better for the experience. I honestly feel that if I slammed the guys for acting "weird" early on, they could easily have abandoned the advisory board, and we would have ended up with sessions run only by the girls. By my being patient, it became a win-win situation for all.

Of course, there are times when boys will cross the line and need to be dealt with as any other disruptive patron. The focus here is to simply attempt to explain teen boys' behaviors, and offer an understanding to librarians of what makes them tick in certain situations.

THE RITE OF PASSAGE INTO MANHOOD?

During the teenage years, many boys have trouble determining what it means to grow up to be a young man. With so many divorces and single parents characterizing the current state of U.S. family life, this confusion may be compounded by an absence of an adult male at home. Many boys are unsure of who they are, who they will become, or even how they should act during their years of puberty. In contrast, girls undergo the physical change of starting their menstruation period, which arguably can be labeled a physical signal that the girls are progressing into womanhood. Girls may wish to present a more mature image emotionally as their bodies physically change from that of a young girl to a woman.

Teenage boys have no such physical benchmark. For many teens in the United States, there is not even a ceremony that suggests to them that its time to become a man. Too often boys struggle to find their true identity and can become something like chameleons. They may even be different personalities on different days.

Internally, teen boys are questioning what type of man should they grow up to be? They may emulate a teacher, a coach, or some other authority figure in their lives such as a policeman or fireman. However, with the booming explosion of video games and graphic novels, many boys gravitate toward being a superhero. This is not to say they are planning to leap tall buildings or become faster than a speeding bullet. They may simply want to be like a superhero appears to them in the popular culture media.

In video games, movies, and comic books, superheroes present a definite message about masculinity and what it takes to be a man. A superhero has a strong jaw that portrays a stoic, unflappable outlook at life and any danger that may come his way. Of course, they are strong and tough. Who else can slug it out with evil villains in the most arduous conditions, often being thrown against, and knocking over, a brick wall? Competitiveness is a constant superhero trait. But the most alluring superhero characteristic that strongly appeals to teenage boys is that superheroes, for the most part, are invincible. Thus, a great way to entice teen males into the library is to build a graphic novel and comic book section. These types of reading materials have become essential to any public library's teen area.

Using a superhero as a role model can possibly translate into the wildly passionate enthusiasm many teenage boys have for professional wrestling.

With a television and cable access, boys can view larger-than-life wrestlers with six-pack abs, vein-popping biceps, and outrageous hair unleash mayhem in the ring—and are seemingly indestructible while doing it! A wise teen librarian makes sure there are books and magazines in the collection about professional wrestling.

Boys unsure of their developing bodies and questioning if they will be strong or weak may be intimidated by the barrage of visual highlights of professional athletes on sports shows. Amazing feats of leaping through the air and viciously slamming a basketball, possessing world-class speed, or achieving a bench press of over 400 pounds bombard young men into possibly thinking that this is what all men should become.

There are role models out there for all boys, but any positive message may be swallowed up by these unreachable types of broad and amazing male performances promoted by the mass media. A teen male may realize he will not ever be what he sees other males achieving on television or on the Internet. The mixed message of what being a man really is may nudge a teenage boy into experiencing feelings of inadequacy, and he may develop subsequent anger, which, in the worst-case scenario, could lead to violence.

This is not to say all boys will contain a boiling rage inside resulting from feelings of not living up to expectations, but it is a distinct possibility. As a teen librarian, how does this struggle of boys establishing themselves intersect with your job performance?

THE BOYS ARE HERE, NOW WHAT?

My first suggestion for you is to consider what might happen if you left the boys alone under the rationale that "they really aren't bothering anyone." I am not suggesting you do this, but consider a possible ripple effect of just leaving them alone. This seems to happen all too frequently with library employees who are thrust into dealing with teens, something that is not their favorite aspect of their job. A prevailing mindset from these employees is that the boys will be fine by themselves, and that they really don't need library assistance. Nothing could be further from the truth.

Most boys are reluctant to ask for help. Males, both adult and teen, tend to want to solve any issue on their own. If your library's atmosphere is one of "let-them-come-to-us," then what will simply happen is that the teen males will be isolated in one area of the library and the employees will be situated behind the floor's help desk. This achieves nothing.

What is needed is for you to connect with all teen patrons, including the boys. Engage them in conversation. Ask some basic reader's advisory questions such as "What do you like to do?" or "What are you into?" You may be surprised. By going to them and asking simple icebreaking questions, you may discover the initial nugget of a great program that will become a huge success. And better yet, a program that will draw boys to the library.

To leave the boys alone makes it easier for them to disconnect. Boys can easily fall into the stereotype of the lone, stoic, tough guy. This does not mean they don't wish to talk to you; they just may not have a concept of how to start the conversation. As a young adult librarian, you need to be proactive and establish yourself as a role model for literacy and reading, especially books and library materials that will appeal to teen males. Let boys know that nonfiction reading counts as reading too, and that their reading tastes are okay. Magazines, newspapers, Web sites, biographies, science books, comic books, and graphic novels are all reading material. They are not violating any standards by reading what they like to read.

On the other hand, you might find a teen guy in your library who is expanding and embracing his newfound maturity. He might be very ambitious. This might be the guy that approaches you and says, "I probably can do this myself, but I want to make sure I am in the right spot." This guy wants to talk. Let him. Switch roles with him and ask him for advice on books. A great question is to ask him, "What book would you recommend to your friends?"

Another guy may come up to you, not ready to discuss book titles, but simply wanting to help. Perhaps he feels the need to flex his developing muscles. Put him to work! Moving tables or setting up chairs for your next program might be a way to gain a loyal teen patron. However, don't just use him as a beast of burden. Ask him what book he would like to see on a display titled "Cool Teen Reads." The single most important thing you can accomplish is to engage teenage boys in conversation. You will also be surprised how adept boys are with laptop and PC computers, DVD players, and LCD projectors. Give them a bit of ownership at your next program and let them set up the electronic equipment. At my anime club, I ask the guys to wire up a DVD player to the television monitor, a fairly simple task. They rush to prove that they have the ability to control the "mysteries" of electronics. I will also give the remote to the guys as we settle in to watch a Japanese cartoon. They love that feeling of power that the gadget provides.

When we leave boys alone, we shortchange their emotional needs. How can we expect them to return to the library if they feel they have been ignored? Another possibility is that behavior problems may come about from their emotional need for attention that is not provided by the staff.

One of the worst mindsets a library can adopt is that boys are misguided females. We as adults tend to want to "fix" boys' behavior and moods. The teacher gene kicks in and we as librarians feel the urge to tell them to behave. Often that is to force them as a square peg into the round hole of acting polite, calm and in control of themselves—in other words—like the girls. Boys view this "correction" of their behavior as forcing them to become feminine or weak. They will most likely rebel against any suggestion of doing so. I often state during workshop presentations that as young adult librarians, we are one of the few public adult authority figures that are not immediately threatening to teens, especially boys. We do not wear uniforms. We do not force them to do things they may not wish to do. They can call us by our first names. Why in the world would we sacrifice this great advantage to connect with teens by immediately slapping down rules and attempting to discipline them?

During their adolescent years, boys view themselves as somewhere between a superhero and a geek. They may be tough, competitive, and consider themselves invincible. Or, they may be completely unsure of who they are and what they will become. The young men are often without a role model of how they should act, and they turn to pop culture media. What they glean from the media is often an outrageous personality that is in immediate conflict with the traditional library atmosphere. As a teen librarian, know all boys are different. Know that their bodies and minds are sending a steady stream of mixed messages. Use this knowledge, not to alienate the teen males, but to better provide quality library services to them. They may reward you with an outstanding lifelong library patron.

FURTHER READING

Brooks, David. "The Gender Gap at School." *New York Times* (June 11, 2006), 4.12.

Glennon, Will. *200 Ways to Raise a Boy's Emotional Intelligence.* Berkeley, CA: Conari Press, 2000.

Gurian, Michael. *Understanding Guys: A Guide for Teenage Girls.* New York: Price Stern Sloan, 1999.

Madaras, Lynda. *The What's Happening to My Body? Book for Boys.* New York: New Market Press, 1984.

Shaffer, Susan Morris & Gordon, Linda Perlman. *Why Boys Don't Talk—And Why It Matters: A Parent's Survival Guide to Connecting with Your Teen.* New York: McGraw-Hill, 2005.

Sommers, Christina Hoff. *The War against Boys: How Misguided Feminism is Harming Our Young Men.* New York: Simon & Schuster, 2000.

Wallis, Claudia. "What Makes Teens Tick." *Time,* Canadian edition (May 10, 2004), 42–49.

Chapter 3

MALES AS READERS: THEIR READING HABITS

Throughout the introduction and opening chapters of this book, it is asserted that young adult males are perhaps the most misunderstood and hard-to-reach patrons using a public or school library. Likewise, I contend that a typical library's collection does not completely satisfy the needs of teen male readers. In order to provide quality service to this unique patron group, you must know and understand the habits of teen male readers and comprehend that these habits and reading tastes change at a rapid pace during the teenage years.

As a young man passes through the teenage years, from a 13-year-old to an 18-year-old, he undergoes profound changes; and rarely do his reading preferences remain the same in those developmental years. Unfortunately, due to several factors many libraries do not keep pace with these rapid reading changes.

In many libraries, the budget for young adult materials is limited or has recently suffered funding cuts. In extreme cases of low funding, the library's young adult librarian may only purchase less expensive paperback titles that are prominently advertised by publishers. Often these hard sell titles are not specifically geared to male reading tastes, but instead target teenage female readers. A recent order catalog promoting young adult titles displays the covers of: *French Kiss*, *Follow Your Heart*, and *Dear*

Dumb Diary. Very few covers of titles with boy-appeal are shown. Fantasy titles that appeal to both sexes, such as Garth Nix's *Drowned Wednesday* are included; but once again, the main emphasis is with books that appeal to female reading tastes.

Additionally, in many YA departments, shelf space is limited, and fiction takes priority over nonfiction (which males generally enjoy). And finally, many public libraries have a close working relationship with the nearby secondary schools and the young adult collection primarily reflects that school's homework assignments, thus becoming an extension of the school curriculum. Reading assigned at schools doesn't take into account specific gender preferences. Instead, it usually focuses on classics and critically acclaimed "literary" books—not exactly at the top of the list for boys. All these factors affect the collection in a potentially guy-unfriendly way and may inadvertently influence boys to shy away from the library, feeling that there is nothing there that immediately interests them.

WHY DO SOME TEEN MALES LOSE INTEREST IN READING?

Constantly changing pop culture influences the teen world and what was in style 7 years ago (a generation to teens) has evolved to new forms of music, clothing, and slang. Images that dominate a teen's daily life are now vastly different from just less than a decade ago and a teen collection needs frequent updating to keep up with the trends, including the must-have current titles broadcasted through the media. Proficient at surfing the Web to locate the most recent, the hottest and coolest things, teen patrons are in tune with the latest popular titles.

Many libraries hang onto books that have "stood the test of time," a concept that contrasts with the principles of a teen world that places prime emphasis on the latest, next-best thing. The music industry brings out new song lists weekly and a vast majority of the song titles target teens. Music stores would turn a small profit if they only featured songs that have stood the test of time. Imagine teen customers' reactions if they were flipping through CDs and only found the top hits of 7 years ago? I imagine there would be several questioning phone calls to the administration if the latest CDs in the music section featured *Candle in the Wind* by Elton John or *Tubthumping* by Chumbawamba, both top songs of less than 10 years ago in 1998. It just doesn't make sense for libraries and librarians to hang onto books that were popular 10 years ago, insisting that teens should develop interest in these titles that have served their time even though their popularity has waned.

Many libraries have begun ambitious initiatives to serve their teen populations, but at times the actual process to achieve these initiatives contrasts starkly with their stated goals. Libraries often purchase and provide materials to young adults in a completely different way than other organizations that serve teens and promote products to them. Although award-winning titles earn their rightful place in teen areas, libraries tend to purchase them *after* the winners are announced, then catalog them and further delay the time it takes for teens to put their hands on the book. Teens crave the newest and freshest items now—that means this minute. Consider including more new releases *before* they appear on award-winning lists. This requires you to consistently read reviews and make sound judgments on titles that will be seriously considered for awards, but your efforts will likely be rewarded.

Further, don't allow a few award-winning titles, especially titles from years gone by, to dominate your collection. Weed and update the teen collection—constantly. Just as a successful music store would never dream of having its inventory dominated by titles produced a teen generation ago, a library's teen collection should also not be focused on award-winning books from even as recent as 7 years ago. Include a healthy balance of new and current titles.

Growing Up in Coal Country by Susan Campbell Bartoletti

Seamstress by Sara Tuvel Bernstein

Tangerine by Edward Bloor

Tenderness by Robert Cormier

Out of the Dust by Karen Hesse

Blood and Chocolate by Annette Curtis Klause

Into Thin Air by Jon Krakauer

Swallowing Stones by Joyce McDonald

Harlem by Walter Dean Myers

Starlite Drive-In by Marjorie Reynolds

1998 Top 10 Best Books for Young Adults
Source: **Accessed from http://www.ala.org/yalsa on February 10, 2006.**

During the teenage years, the focus on reading, and often the only influence about reading, is the reading introduced by schools, whether through a school assignment requiring research or a selection from a fiction required reading list.

Boys crave action and want to do things. Poetic prose, lush descriptive passages, or character development hold little interest for most young male readers. If they must read, they prefer to read about something that excites them; and books from school assignments usually don't fulfill these criteria. According to Michael Smith and Jeffrey Wilhelm authors of *Reading Don't Fix No Chevys: Literacy in the Lives of Young Men*, reluctant readers in the classroom setting—older boys who called themselves nonreaders—actually read voraciously outside of the academic setting to pursue their personal interests and goals. In other words, they don't hate reading. They just hate what they had to read at school (Halls 2005). Some examples of report topics that I have fielded requests for from teen males include "Any Important Person Famous for His or Her Work for Civil Rights," "The Symbolism in Hawthorne's *The Scarlet Letter*," "Presidential Scandals Throughout History," and "The Social Life of the Ancient Greeks." These assignments require reading to earn the desired passing grade, but they are hardly the stimulus that will turn boys onto reading.

Of course, girls are assigned the same or similar topics, but it is common knowledge that girls read more than boys. Don't these dry report topics turn girls off of reading also? And why do girls so often turn to fiction for reading pleasure while guys often turn away from novels? There may not be a clear-cut answer to these questions. My opinion is that girls are more accepting of reading (and assignments) than boys. Again, a strong influence is school.

Besides report topics, schools often either publish a recommended reading list (often for summer reading), or assign books to read as a class reading assignment. These book titles that are chosen by the classroom teacher are often tried and true classics, in which the writing has been deemed to enable solid teaching. This list includes titles such as *The Scarlet Letter*, *The Old Man and the Sea*, or *The Lord of the Flies*. Assigning these types of titles and *only* these titles sends a message to teens, and especially male teens who are already apprehensive about assigned books, that reading is work, and that you should learn or gain something from the effort. Often the assigned titles feature strong characters, and the plot is character-driven, a feature that usually appeals more to girls then boys. So although a school's or teacher's intentions may include the lofty goal of appreciating quality literature, the structure of the assignment may be inadvertently alienating boys from becoming avid readers.

Quick 5	*Lord of the Flies* by William Golding
	A Separate Peace by John Knowles
	To Kill a Mockingbird by Harper Lee
	Red Badge of Courage by Stephen Crane
	The Scarlet Letter by Nathaniel Hawthorne

Five Traditional Fiction Titles Commonly Assigned in School
*Note***: These traditional class reads have annually been assigned by schools in the service area of public libraries where I have been employed as a young adult librarian.**

Due to its nature, reading is a physically passive act, something that just does not require the fast or strong motor movements that characterize boys during their teenage years. While on duty at a public library help desk, I've informally observed the use of computers with Internet access and usually it is the boys who are rapidly surfing the Web using the mouse or arrow keys to search sports sites or play online video games. At the same time (for the most part) girls are often observed being more interested in

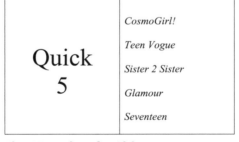

Five Magazines for Girls

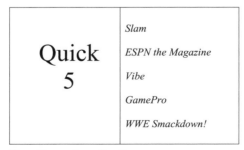

Five Magazines for Guys

casual reading and can be seen leafing through and discussing teen magazines such as *Glamour*, *YM*, and *J-14*.

From what I have observed over the years, guys need action stimulus, and the passive nature of reading does not fulfill that need. Currently boys find the action they crave through manipulating a computer keyboard.

But the act of reading isn't the only factor that discourages young males from reading. Limited selection of reading materials can also turn guys off. Make sure your library includes materials for guys; and help your library administrator understand the bias toward female readers in your collection, and how to overcome it.

The publishing world also participates in the imbalance of reading materials. In his book *Beyond the Pale*, author Marc Aronson includes a chapter with the title "Why Adults Can't Read Boy Readers," Aronson states that the book world, including publishers, neglects the reading needs of boys and continues to produce and promote books that do not meet the needs of boys, i.e., fiction, poetry, and folktales. He states, "Until we as adults recognize this gap in literature we create, we will not be able to respond to the aching needs of boy readers" (Aronson 2003).

BOYS AS RELUCTANT READERS

The old saying goes, "Boys Will Be Boys." Seemingly this is a statement advising adults to just let boys grow up and they will be fine. This mindset was challenged by an article published in *Newsweek* entitled "The Trouble With Boys." According to statistics, across the nation and in every demographic, boys are falling further and further behind in school. High-school boys are losing ground to girls on standardized writing tests. The article goes on to say that the number of boys who said they didn't like school rose 71 percent between 1980 and 2001, according to a University of Michigan study (*Newsweek*, January 30, 2006).

Pay close attention to this information. Males, especially teen males, often do not immediately come to mind as a group to consider in collection development, programming, and readers' advisory. As previously noted, the emphasis has traditionally been on services and books that appeal to females, who make up the higher percentage of teen patrons. This contributes to a vicious cycle. I believe the crisis referred to earlier of boys falling behind in school is linked to the shortcomings of libraries in serving males, a situation that may breed reluctant readers. And that not liking to read causes boys to perform poorly in educational environments.

Defining Reluctant Readers

What is a reluctant reader? The initial sentence of the purpose statement for YALSA's (Young Adult Library Services Association) Quick Picks for Reluctant Young Adult Readers Committee states, "The list is for young adults (ages 12–18) who, for whatever reasons, do not like to read (Quick Picks—to view the entire Quick Picks lists dating back to 1996, check YALSA's Web site, http://www.ala.org/yalsa). Of course, the list consists of books recommended for both boys and girls. However, according to Michael Sullivan, author of the article, "Why Johnny Won't Read," studies have shown that on average boys read less than girls (Sullivan 2004). Of course, due to the scope of this book, this chapter focuses on young adult boys as reluctant readers.

Keep in mind that "reluctant readers" does not necessarily mean non-readers or teens unable to read. Reluctant readers are teenagers who can read but choose not to for a variety of reasons. They do not come from any single background or mold. A reluctant reader may be a student who does quite well on standardized tests, but has not come across a book that is worth taking him away from his valuable free time. On the other hand, perhaps the teen has the ability to read, but struggles with vocabulary; and therefore chooses not to, due to the difficulty the task presents. Other males (and females) may just not feel that reading is exciting enough for their interests.

The list of factors contributing to a teen becoming a reluctant reader is seemingly endless. He or she may not be subjected to a proper reading environment at home, or at school. It comes as no surprise that school systems, and the overall education offered in each system, varies from community to community. In some rural areas as well as in some of the more populated urban centers of the country, poor education is the culprit. Reading may be simply too much of a struggle for a handicapped teen lacking access to proper equipment to enhance his or her reading efforts. Teens with ADD, or with personal or emotional problems, struggle as well. So you can see how the list of factors contributing to teens choosing not to read is actually endless.

Examining the causes of teen reluctant readers is not the focus of this book, but it is important to recognize the diversity of factors that contribute to the situation. The focus here is on things you as a librarian can change and control, that is, book selection, book promotion, library programming, and an overall atmosphere that welcomes teens of all reading tastes and levels.

In this chapter we specifically address reluctant readers who choose not to read for pleasure (students not choosing to read curriculum assignments is another matter altogether).

In the *Newsweek* article mentioned earlier, we are introduced to Nikolas Arnold, age 15, and a sophomore in Santa Monica, California. We learn that this young man has always been an advanced reader, but his grades are erratic. Last semester, his English teacher assigned two girls' favorites, *Memoirs of a Geisha* and *The Secret Life of Bees*. Nikolas got a D (*Newsweek*, January 30, 2006). When working with teen readers be sure to include books that appeal to guys. Throughout this book you'll find many suggestions for both fiction and nonfiction guy-friendly titles.

The *Newsweek* article also refers to Michael Thompson and his documentary video, *Raising Cain*. Thompson summarizes that boys often measure themselves by one simple item. They will ask themselves, "Does this make me look weak?" From what we know about boys, we can assume that if they feel a situation makes them look weak, they will choose to not place themselves in that situation. Having to make a reading choice from a list of titles with high girl appeal can easily cause a male to feel he looks weak or feminine. The *Newsweek* article continues, "That's part of the reason that videogames have such a powerful hold on boys: the action is constant, they can calibrate just how hard the challenges will be and, when they lose, the defeat is private" (*Newsweek*, January 30, 2006).

Engaging Reluctant Readers

From the results of these recent alarming studies you may think that there is no hope for boys to become readers. Not true. However, you must go beyond simply having books that appeal to guys on the library shelves. Promote those books through your teen Web site, in a floor display or during a school visit booktalk. And perhaps most importantly, *read* books that interest boys—don't just borrow a list from a journal or a listserv. If you can demonstrate that you honestly think a guy book is cool, then boys are more likely to open up to your other book suggestions. Remember, a reluctant reader's choices are probably going to be selective; and will most likely include titles that are not recognized as high literary works of writing. This does not mean that boys' reading tastes should be labeled as inferior.

I have sat in on many informal discussions about the outstanding recent title releases—over dinner with people from all over the country and during national conventions. During these discussions, I have realized that many female professionals, who have great insight into reading and books, have something in common with teen male readers. The two demographic groups—adult female book people and teen males—often don't particularly care for what the other group likes to read. I've also attended many workshops at statewide, regional, and national levels, where recommended books for young adults are presented. Inevitably, the discussion and presentation of titles centers around the character development in the book, rather than the story, or any action that happens inside the book. Adults often passionately voice their opinions about how the story's characters reacted to each other and how they changed during the book. Reluctant readers, both male and female, eventually lose interest in a title (no matter how highly recommended it is by a professional) if they feel that "nothing is happening" or they "don't get the point." Reluctant readers have little patience for lengthy descriptions of a character's inner emotional turmoil.

Consider vampire novels. Girls might tolerate long, tension-filled descriptions of how the girl feels as the vampire slowly breaks her resistance and draws her to him. Boys want the vampire to bite her neck and have the blood begin to flow as quickly as possible. Thus the sexual attraction between a high school girl and a male vampire detailed in Stephenie Meyer's wonderful *Twilight* draws girls to the story. Guys, on the other hand, would rather read vampire stories laced with blood splatters such as the *Cirque du Freak* series by Darren Shan.

Now you may be asking yourself, will boys reject all of my best efforts to introduce them to books, and discuss literature? The answer is no. Boys want to talk about their reading experiences, but on their own terms. In classes where students are separated by sex, as they are in the youth development center that I visit about every 3 weeks, the boys are much more open with me than the girls seem to be (interestingly, in both rural and city schools across the nation, experimental classrooms separating boys and girls are being tested in hopes of improving educational achievement. You'll find suggestions for further reading on this topic listed at the end of this chapter.) Perhaps they crave a male presence that is missing in their lives. Or, the connection can simply be labeled "male bonding," in which the young men find a comfort zone with my presence. Whatever the reason, the boys eagerly and openly share with me how exciting a climatic scene was or how cool a nonfiction book was that hit home with them. The girls, on the other hand, tell me the book was "all right." I've learned two things from these experiences. One, it is important to know your audience when promoting books—particularly, if the demographic is more male or female. Bring books that appeal to the group you're speaking to. The second lesson I've learned is to be honest with the teens. Let them know that a certain book is particularly appealing to girls, where others appeal to boys. Spend equal time promoting both books for boys and also others for girls, alternating titles if possible.

The bad news is that half of your audience may not be interested in a particular book. On the other hand, I have had success introducing girls to such high guy-appeal books such as the Cirque du Freak series mentioned earlier simply by saying before talking about the book, "This is more of a guy book." Some girls will perk up upon hearing that phrase. On the other hand, if told, "This is a girls' book," most often the boys immediately lose interest.

Identifying Books for Reluctant Teen Male Readers

How can you recognize the titles that male teens love—the ones that will change a male reluctant reader into a reader? That is a very good question. YALSA's Quick Picks' list is a good starting point. Selected annually, this list includes books for both male and females, so not all of the titles will appeal to guys. Also keep in mind that 12-year-old reluctant readers don't have the same interests when they turn 18.

Furthermore, there are certain general characteristics that appeal to male reluctant readers; if you find books with these characteristics, you have books that your reluctant readers could very well enjoy.

BOOK SELECTION GUIDELINES FOR TEEN MALE RELUCTANT READERS

You may not have time to field test titles before or after they are placed on your shelves. For avid readers, this is not so much of an issue. They will find their favorite authors and titles and know their way around library shelves. But for a reluctant, or discriminating reader, things are different. They have to buy into, or be "sold" the book before they even pick it up to examine it. Most librarians enter the profession as readers and readers who read voraciously. To choose books that will appeal to a teen male (or female) that chooses not to read requires a different approach.

It All Starts with the Cover

A cover for a book that attracts male reluctant readers conveys some degree of excitement and possibly danger. A photograph of a wild skateboard stunt, a full-color representation of a horrifying creature from a drawing book, or an above-the-rim photograph of an NBA dunk are just a few examples of cover illustrations that attract guys. Photographs are more apt to engage male readers than line drawings or cheesy and dated hand-drawn illustrations (the exception here is graphic novels). And don't forget the back covers. Flipping over Joseph Delaney's *The Last Apprentice: Revenge of the Witch* (New York: Greenwillow, 2005), readers immediately notice a teaser, "Warning! Not to be read after dark. Especially page 148." Now what page do you think readers will open to first?

The title font comes into play also. Is it edgy? Gothic looking? Does it come across as bold, and have an impact? Does it have attitude? A rough-looking font style clicks in a guy's mind.

Three wonderful examples of edgy title fonts appear on covers of the ninth book in the Cirque du Freak series by Darren Shan, *Killers of the Dawn* (New York: Little, Brown, 2005); *The Ruins of Gorlan: The Ranger's Apprentice* (New York: Philomel Books, 2005) by John Flanagan; and *Scorpia* (New York: Philomel Books, 2005) by Anthony Horowitz. These bold title fonts pack a punch, immediately drawing the eyes to the book. Boys become curious about the potential danger awaiting readers that the artwork and title fonts suggest. On the other hand, if the cover art or font is perceived as curvy, flowery, or flowing, then guys immediately shrug that book off as being more suited for girls.

Does the book blurb on the back confuse the reader with complications between the characters? Or does it tease with just enough plot detail? Does it hint at action and adventure, or does it emphasize the relationships between the characters? The back cover of Walter Dean Myers' novel, *Monster* (New York: HarperCollins, 1999) boldly states on a black background, "Steve Harmon's black. He's in jail, maybe forever. He's on trial for murder. And he's sixteen years old" (Myers 1999).

On the inside flap of Adam Meyer's book, *The Last Domino* (New York: G. P. Putnam's Sons, 2005), you'll find these two sentences: "Daniel teaches Travis to stand up, fight back, and go after what he wants most. But their relationship develops into a combustible friendship—one where manipulation leads Travis to violent extremes" (Meyer 2005). This is a great hook for guys—with multiple hints at action.

For Fiction: Does the First Page Excite?

A great opening sentence tells a male reader that there is danger ahead. The first page explains the danger further, and adds even more problems. Male reluctant readers want to know who the main character is, and as soon as possible, what are the problems that lie ahead for that character. Male readers generally accept a character growing emotionally over the course of an exciting story. However, to assure holding the male reader's interest, the main character should be delineated in the first few opening pages, if not the very first page.

For Fiction: Do the First 10 Pages Set the Pace?

If you know that a particular guy is reluctant to read a book, then you cannot expect him to donate his time to read ten pages where nothing happens but lengthy poetic descriptions of the setting or how the main character feels at that time. For male reluctant readers, there must be action, or at the very least, "a rattling of sabers" anticipating action. Ask yourself, has the problem for the main character been defined? Is the antagonist portrayed in the first 10 pages? Has the first confrontation between enemies taken place? If so, then let the reading begin.

For Fiction: Does the Book Follow through with the Initial Suggestion?

If the male reader is hooked, does the rest of the book move at a fast enough clip to compel him to read more? Does it bog down with excessive description? Are dangerous situations placed at regular intervals? Do the majority of chapters end with a cliffhanger? Does the dialogue resonate with what the male reader feels is realistic? Male readers drop like hot potatoes books that contain slang that is dated, stilted, or out of place.

For Fiction: White Space

To increase the pace of turning pages, many publishers have become liberal with "white space," intermixing it throughout the book with wide margins, more space between lines, and larger type sizes. Chapters may begin down a third of the length of the page. A chapter may end with only two or three lines on a page, leaving the rest of the page blank. White space allows a reluctant reader to keep reading, and keep his eyes traveling to the next thing. He (or she) does not get bogged down in a repetitive left to right eye movement where each page is a solid block of text. Compare young adult novels of 15 years ago to a title released in 2006. You'll likely see that the format of the two texts differ greatly, with the 2006 title having much more white space.

For Nonfiction: Does the Inside Content Support the Cover?

So your book has a great, and reader-enticing cover. Will the reader see similar illustrations inside? If so, are they in color? Or does the book have a great cover and then turn into a "textbook" when the reluctant reader flips through the pages? A book illustrated by only black and white line drawings does not appeal to teenage boys. Reluctant readers are also experts at taking a quick glance at a page and evaluating if reading the block text format will take up too much of their time. I have often seen a book set aside accompanied by the words, "Man, that's a lot of reading."

For Nonfiction: Does the Book Have Interesting Sections Throughout?

Many guys do not like to read repetitively left to right and top to bottom across the pages. They prefer to let their eyes bounce around the page. A nonfiction book for teen male readers addresses this reading style through text that is interspersed with illustrations, bulleted lists, call-outs, and information boxes.

Illustrations (preferably color photographs) should dominate the space on a page with explanations appearing right next to them. Many nonfiction titles fail to explain the illustration. A good nonfiction title for guys is one where they can open to any page and be rewarded with something that interests them on the topic, and where they can see a visual example of what they are reading about.

For teen male readers, the more reading options per page, the better— nonfiction books should be similar to a Web site in appearance. In her book, *Radical Change: Books for Youth in a Digital Age*, author Eliza T. Dresang comments, "Children of the digital age are not disturbed by non-linear narrative. They encounter it every day" (Dresang 1999). This simple scale is a quick and easy way to determine if a book has reluctant reader appeal.

---

1. The cover, by artwork or title font, somehow draws the teen male to the book.

2. The cover or blurb prompts him to open the book and he begins reading.

3. He is hooked early and the book moves at a fast pace.

4. He finishes the book! Or, in the case of a nonfiction title, he spends time examining the book.

5. He shares the book with his friends and it moves around by word of mouth.

Determining Reluctant Reader Appeal

If these criteria are met, you can be assured that book has guy-reluctant reader appeal. If the reader doesn't get past step number 2, then that book has something about it that turns guy reluctant readers off. It may be a title more suited to avid readers. Remember, if a guy perceives that the act of reading makes him look weak, he will not read. If the book is a good one, and he shares it with his friends, then he is moving out of his private mode. The teen is confident his friends will not ridicule him over the title, a trait that makes the particular book pretty cool.

The world of reluctant readers is constantly changing. While reluctant readers normally do not want to be bogged down with thick books, they will accept lengthier titles IF the content speaks to them. With the widespread hoopla over Harry Potter, teens (and to some extent reluctant reader teens) have become more accepting of longer books than they were about 7 or 8 years ago (before *Harry Potter and the Sorcerer's Stone* was released). In my opinion, it is difficult to place a page limit on what kind of book attracts a reluctant reader. With large amounts of white space throughout a book, publishers have created fast-moving titles that may have up to 300 pages, but the printing format holds the interest of the reader. Teachers who try to force reading by demanding a selected book have more than 200 pages, should reevaluate their thinking. It is entirely possible that a 300-page book can be a quick read. Conversely, a book with less than 150 pages may turn out to be incredibly deep and complicated.

GUY-APPEALING CONTENT

You can get a good idea of what appeals to teen males by simply engaging males in library activities. This is also one of the main ways to engage teen males in reading. The trick is to somehow get the guys to enter the library, so you can begin quizzing them about their reading interests. This dilemma is discussed at length in Chapter 7, which addresses how teen males can take part in library programming and teen advisory boards.

Use the Quick Pick list as a guide to reluctant reader subjects for males, remembering that the list is made by librarians who have field-tested nominated titles with teens in their own service areas. A book that has high male appeal in New York City may not be the best selection to bring guys into the building for a rural library in Ohio. When selecting books for your young adult area, consider your community and your patrons' specific interests before blindly ordering a particular book from a nationally produced recommended list.

What follows are a few subject areas that have in the past attracted male reluctant readers to books or other reading materials.

Violence or at Least the Threat of Violence

Physical violence is a fascination for boys. Reading about the dangerous act of putting yourself in harm's way while nearby someone is being hurt or killed produces a thrill for many male teens. Reading about war, gang violence, or even books with photos of football collisions are good examples of the types of brutality that appeal to boys.

Sex or at Least the Threat of Sex

Teen males are curious about their sexual feelings and attractions. This is something brand new in their lives and they wonder about their own sexual attractiveness and the possibility of experiencing sex. Putting themselves in the place of a male character about to connect with another teen can be the next best thing to sex.

Vampires or at Least the Threat of Vampires

All monsters are cool to boys, but the stealth and cunning of vampires holds a special allure, to say nothing of the blood. Toss into the mix that vampires, by their icy stares, can render women helpless, well, there you have it. Vampires can be victims themselves, for example someone who has been turned by being bitten and has no choice in the matter. Or they can be the main biter or leader in the coven of vampires. Either way, it doesn't matter to teen boys. What they don't want to read about is the romance of vampires. They want a high body count and lots of suspense.

Vehicles with Internal Combustion Engines

The most important birthday to many a teenage guy is not the far-off eighteenth or the even more distant twenty-first, but the within-reach sixteenth birthday. That is when he can first break the shackles of servitude to his parents by borrowing the family car and achieving brief flights of freedom. Guys love to daydream about the hottest vehicles, and being behind the wheel while cruising their paved stomping grounds. If girls sneak a peek at them, why, that is a bonus.

Popular Culture

It's hip to be cool and in the know. Inside their sarcastic exterior, many teenage boys actually hold a high level of self-doubt. Knowing what is interesting to the rest of the crowd is very important. Coolness can go out of style quickly, so guys often get their pop culture fix from browsing magazines and order many subscriptions on a wide variety of current topics—from sports and entertainment to celebrities and the arts.

How-to-Draw Books, Especially Cartooning Titles

Today's boys have always known a huge number and variety of television cartoons. Drawing what they see and adding their own spin to an imaginary creature is a great way for them to express themselves. And, since there are no grades for this type of drawing, any failure is simply in their own mind. There are hundreds of great drawing books out there featuring monsters, villains, machines, or practically anything a boy would want to draw.

Nonfiction Sports Books

Boys today are bombarded by images of sports. Their senses are assaulted from billboards to 24/7 coverage on television. The message?

Dunking a basketball, spinning away from a tackler into the end zone and whacking a fastball out of the park are majestic feats. Of course, most teen males normally understand they probably are not capable of achieving these feats, so the next best thing is to read about them. Buy lots of glossy sports books with photographs that take up an entire page. Boys will thank you.

REACHING OUT TO TEEN MALE READERS

For generations teenage boys have taken part in activities that are driven by action. In the first half of the twentieth century, before television, boys were actively more involved in outdoor activities and released energy through loosely organized team sports, hunting, or fishing: things that required movement. When used automobiles became affordable, teenaged boys began to mechanically tinker and modify the cars into hot-rods. Today, to fulfill the need to explore and create by doing, boys often turn to video games, entering imaginary worlds that are there to conquer just by using their hands.

However, sometime during the teen years, a teacher, the school curriculum, or a librarian requires boys to abstain from these activities that interest them and to "curl up with a good book" and imagine themselves as a character in a story. Is it any wonder why boys sigh with exasperation when receiving reading assignments?

As a member of monthly book discussion groups that include adults who work closely with teens (school and public librarians and teachers), I am often surprised to receive questions about "teaching" the book or "how can we use this in a lesson?" The books that often prompt the best discussions among professionals are character-driven novels, often featuring a female character such as Jennifer Donnelly's *A Northern Light* or Joyce Carol Oates' *Freaky Green Eyes*, two examples that sparked hours of debate about the characters' strong and weak points. However wonderful these novels are, if a balance of a guy book is not presented to teens by the school personnel, there is an immediate disconnect. And where are the young men to go to find reading materials that interest them?

To balance character-driven novels with deep introspection, look for titles that meet the male need to explore and conquer, if not with their bodies, then by challenging their imaginations with thrilling action on the pages. Anthony Horowitz has created the Alex Rider Series, titles that feature suspense, action, and each chapter is a cliffhanger. Several recent sports books include extremely realistic scenes. For example, the football action in John Coy's *Crackback* is very well done. Sports scenes are superbly written in Carl Deuker's *Night Hoops* about basketball, and in Mike Lupica's book, *Heat* featuring baseball. Paul Volponi has created a very realistic basketball world featuring inner city hoops in his book, *Black and White.*

Many boys are drawn to the creepy content of horror novels, especially those that pit a teen male battling supernatural evil *all by himself.* Teen boys who manipulated toy vehicles as children are naturally drawn to Philip Reeve's book *Mortal Engines* where cities travel on huge caterpillar treads.

Hope for these teenage male readers can also be found in graphic novels, a format filled with action and bursting with thrilling illustrations as good battles evil in each panel. Particularly appealing to boys are American comics featuring superheroes such as Spiderman, The Justice League of America, Batman, The Hulk, The Fantastic Four, The Ultimate X-Men– the list goes on and on. Inside the pages, boys can place themselves in situations where the larger-than-life heroes use their strength to battle evil. As they read these adventures, boys are vicariously *doing things* and conquering worlds; reading has taken them there. Many video games are designed on this comic book theme of larger-than-life figures battling with their bodies and confronting "the bad guys."

Action also is abundant in the manga form of graphic novels originating from Asian markets. Once again, boys can picture themselves in the middle of action of such popular graphic novel series such as *Vagabond, Inu Yasha, Initial D*, or *GTO (Great Teacher Onisuka).*

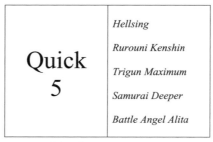

Quick 5	Hellsing
	Rurouni Kenshin
	Trigun Maximum
	Samurai Deeper
	Battle Angel Alita

Manga Titles for Guys

Even with the noblest of intentions about books, and awareness that boys' reading needs differ from girls, educators can still cause male teens to take a detour from the reading highway. Teachers and school librarians often view novels as another tool to illustrate a teaching lesson. I have copresented joint booktalks with a teacher who is very up-to-date with the most popular young adult novels. As he presented different books, his teaching background influence came through and I heard him say statements such as, "There is so much you can learn from a story like this."

On the other hand, representing the public library, I found myself introducing books with phrases like, "You'll love this book because it is so intense!" We both had great books to share with the teens, but my friend's influence was more enthusiastically received by the girls, who may have been more serious about schoolwork, looking for a book where the characters grow and learn. The boys were drawn to the nonfiction titles and the fiction selections that "sounded cool." Books the boys liked included the very visual Dorling Kindersley title *Ultimate Special Forces*, fiction titles *Acceleration* by Graham McNamee and *Full Tilt* by Neal Shusterman, along with *Dr. Ernest Drake's Dragonology*—in other words, titles that are illustrated and more driven by vivid action scenes than dialogue and the interaction of characters. These books also feature cool covers that drew the boys' attention hinting of action and danger, or both. If you're not already aware of Dorling Kindersley Publishing, take a look at the publication of this company that consistently produces many highly visual nonfiction titles on topics such as sports, history, animals, and pop culture. Previews of titles can be accessed at the publisher's Web site, http://www.dk.com.

Anthony Horowitz, author of the previously mentioned Alex Rider series, summarizes the struggles many boys experience in school in Jon Scieszka's book, *Guys Write for Guys Read*. Horowitz talks about daydreaming in class as a 12-year-old, not paying attention to French lessons, and instead thinking of action-filled adventures such as uncovering his teacher as a spy. He comments, "But if you ask me what it was like to be a guy . . . well, for me, doing badly at school was part of the answer. I hated school. But I still enjoy the dreams" (Scieszka 2005).

It has been my privilege to present booktalks in a county juvenile detention center, a place where it was easy to gauge the different reactions to books by males and females. In the gym, I speak to over a 100 teens housed there. Since boys and girls are not allowed to intermingle, the boys are seated on one side of the room and the girls on the other, the two sexes separated by an aisle. The biggest reaction to a book's description from the girls came following my booktalk of *The First Part Last* by Angela Johnson and the girls vocally demanded to know what happened to the characters as they struggle to deal with teen pregnancy and parenthood. I assumed the young men were not at all interested as they slouched in their chairs. The guys showed much more interest in the book, *In the Paint: Tattoos of the NBA and the Stories Behind Them* by leaning forward in their chairs and after the talk, they wanted to flip through the book to figure out which player had the coolest tattoo. The girls were enthusiastic about a fiction book featuring relationships, and the boys were turned on by a very visual nonfiction title.

Encouraging Teen Males to Become Lifelong Readers

A library's service begins with its collection. To keep a teenage male interested in the library, your young adult collection must feature books that interest guys as well as girls. Don't limit your collection to a traditional title startup collection. Include some current titles, making the area fluid and reflecting the pop culture interests of today's teens. Most importantly, include titles that reflect the reading tastes of teen males.

Like any other patron, a male teen will return to the library if, after entering the building, he finds things that interest him. If what he is seeking is not there (or not visible), he will go to a retail bookstore or a comic book shop to find his type of materials. To meet a young man's reading needs, your teen collection should include titles selected from these general types of books:

- Readable nonfiction—not just nonfiction that supports a school curriculum

  Ripley's Believe It or Not, How to Survive a Robot Uprising: Defending Yourself Against the Coming Rebellion by Daniel Wilson, and *Graffiti World: Street Art from Five Continents* by Nicholas Ganz are good examples of readable nonfiction that were not created for strictly research purposes.

- Action-packed fiction

  Soldier Boys by Dean Hughes, *Raven's Gate* by Anthony Horowitz, and *Maximum Ride* by James Patterson are fast-moving novels loaded with danger.

- Horror novels

  Killing Britney by Sean Olin, *Lord Loss* by Darren Shan, and *Peeps* by Scott Westerfeld are books laced with truly gruesome content.

- Graphic novels

  Fullmetal Alchemist, Deathnote, and *Hellsing* are manga series with high guy-appeal. *Teen Titans, X-Men*, and *The Goon* are Western graphic novels series that attract boys.

- Magazines based on subjects that appeal to teen males

  Subscribe to *Revolver, Fangoria*, and *NewType*. These magazines include pop culture topics that will hook teen males.

Literature-Based Programs

Although book selection is vital to attracting male teens, it is not the sole reason for a teenage male to enter the library. As stated earlier, libraries are investing hours of time and thousands of dollars to construct programs to attract patrons. These programs range from a make it-take it Valentine's Day card, ice cream sundae making, to line dancing. Promoting programs that appeal mainly to females is the equivalent of constructing the teen book collection only with female character-driven novels.

What programs does your library offer teens? The vast majority of teen programs I have noticed in libraries are geared to girls or they are somewhat unisex such as ACT/SAT study help or College Financial Aid programs. Thankfully, this is beginning to change. On listservs and in print newsletters, I have recently noticed an increased effort to attract young men to the library through such programs as paintball demonstrations, motocross motorcycle and 4-wheeler safety, NASCAR race car displays, anime film festivals, and cartooning workshops.

These programs can bring males into the library. Your next step is to promote reading at these programs. For example, during your anime club meeting where you view recent anime videos with teens, be sure to have the latest manga books set out for the group to browse and read. There are dozens of how-to-draw books that can be displayed at the door before the cartoonist begins his demonstrations at a cartooning workshop program. Any program can be a catalyst to learning more and reading promotion.

Go Where the Boys Are

In today's changing public libraries, young adult librarians are not expected to simply remain in the building anticipating young adults to approach them for homework help, reader's advisory, or research direction. Of course, many libraries experience after-school crowds of teens entering the building. Young adult librarians are expected to provide programs for these teens to "keep them busy." If you want to reach more teenage boys, take a proactive role and connect with organizations that serve teenage males.

If you're not already making visits to your local middle, junior, and high schools to give booktalks and do other literature promotions, start doing so now. Detention centers, drug rehabilitation centers, the local Boy Scout troop, and recreation centers are other prime organizations with connections to teen males. Most of these groups have either an outreach or an education coordinator. I have had success simply using the telephone book to find an initial contact. A community directory is also a helpful tool for locating contact information. The directory may even include a brief mission statement about the organization. From that information, you can determine whether teen males will be drawn to that organization.

FICTION BOOKS—NOT JUST THE HARDY BOYS ANYMORE

Several generations of male readers trace their first introduction to young adult literature back to Frank and Joe Hardy, sons of detective Fenton Hardy. The intrepid brothers continue to solve crimes to this day. Why? The success of this series can be attributed to story characteristics that have remained central to series titles throughout the entire history of the Hardy Boys. Teen boys love to read about the extreme danger, a crime that has been committed, teens outwitting adult villains, physical action, using motor vehicles and technological gadgetry. The Hardy brothers, trustworthy, reliable boys, keep cool heads when caught in tight spots. These noble traits are what teenage boys have wished to emulate for decades.

Today's young adult books for boys differ from the Hardy Boys' adventures of the 1950s. In the last 25 years, young adult fiction has become increasingly "edgy." The main reading attractions for teenage boys now are found in the genre of realistic fiction, followed by science fiction and fantasy. However, many of the current teen novels feature the same characteristics that have made the Hardy Boys such an enduring presence in young adult literature.

The integrity of the Hardy Boys can still be found in today's more edgy young adult literature geared to male readers, although it is rephrased as "doing the right thing." In Ben Mikaelsen's *Touching Spirit Bear*, Cole physically assaults a classmate and is forced to learn tough lessons on survival and acceptance after he chooses to be isolated on an island to search for his inner self in an attempt to control his anger management problem. Attacked by a bear, the teen almost dies due to his self-centered refusal to accept direction in doing the right things.

Steve Harmon is scared he may be placed in prison for life or even executed for hanging with the wrong crowd after his supposed friends sell him out to the police. On trial for murder, Steve copes with fear and realizes why he made wrong decisions. These are powerful themes in

Walter Dean Myers' *Monster*, a compelling book that urban males can relate to on many levels.

Nate, the 16-year-old protagonist in Janet McDonald's *Brother Hood* attempts to switch personas as he moves between a private academy and the Harlem streets where he lives. Trying too hard to fit in, Nate joins up with his friends as they steal merchandise, making a terribly wrong decision.

In the suspense novel, *Acceleration* by Graham Mcnamee, 17-year-old Duncan tries to right a wrong decision he made years earlier as he tries to prevent a serial killer from killing a targeted woman on the Toronto subway. Listening to his conscience, he finds a certain level of inner courage by tracing the killer back to a locked cellar in the murderer's home.

While their characters are perhaps not entirely as consistently noble as the Hardy Boys, the above titles are far more readable for today's young men and provide positive examples of growing into manhood by doing the right thing. Each of the authors does a wonderful job of providing a "lesson-learned" story without falling into the literary trap of becoming moralistic or overly didactic.

Use of technological gadgets has traveled from the Hardy Boys into the twenty-first century and beyond as well, in young adult literature exemplified in the *Artemis Fowl* series (*Artemis Fowl, The Arctic Incident, The Eternity Code*, and *The Opal Deception*) by Eoin Colfer. Middle school boy readers are drawn to Artemis and his genius for using or developing the perfect electronic device to help him through any situation. Never mind that in the beginning of the series, Artemis uses his intelligence for criminal intent. Boys still are thrilled that a fellow male can outwit and dominate many adult authority figures.

The same male readers may be attracted to the Alex Rider series (*Stormbreaker, Point Blank, Skeleton Key, Eagle Strike, Scorpia*, and *Ark Angel*) by Anthony Horowitz where Alex is recruited by MI5 to become a teen secret agent similar to a young James Bond. Before confronting evil villains, Alex is introduced to cutting-edge weapons and equipment that free him from dangerous situations.

These examples offer you a simple transition for teenage boys with superior techie skills to become interested in a young adult novel featuring extreme gadgetry.

The notions of fair play and respecting one's opponent, themes prevalent in the Hardy Boys' competitions, have moved into today's young adult literature as well, albeit with some new twists. Using the sport as a means not an end to the story, today's young adult sports' novels feature teens caught in emotional situations expounded by their participation in that sport.

Following his father's suicide and his family moving to a poorer section of the city, pitcher Shane Hunter purposely fires a fastball at the head of an opposing batter to release his pent-up anger; and then tries to make amends with the injured batter. *High Heat* by Carl Deuker is an outstanding sports story featuring teen boys from vastly different economical situations pitted against each other in a highly charged situation.

In Rich Wallace's *Wrestling Sturbridge*, Ben struggles with the decision to rat out a teammate who has beaten him in the same weight class, making Ben second string. Discovering that his teammate parties hard on the weekend, Ben has to make the choice of blowing the whistle and becoming a starter or keeping quiet and allowing his teammate to win a state championship.

Although these two titles feature quality writing about sports action, they also show how teens involved in a sport are often confronted with more than just playing the game.

A half century ago, drugs were something that smugglers hid and sold; and at times drugs were a component of the Hardy Boys' mysteries. In today's young adult books, teenage boys are confronted with the decision to use drugs or witness someone close to them using illegal substances.

The serious issues of drug and alcohol addiction and the character's denial of a problem are prevailing themes of Jay Murray's *Bottled Up*. The novel is about Pip, a teen male, living only to get high regardless of the mixed role model message he is sending to his younger brother.

When his idolized older brother quits baseball and becomes a daily user of marijuana in Patricia McCormick's book *My Brother's Keeper*, 13-year-old Toby takes it upon himself to keep the family together by not letting his divorced mother know about the drug habit. Toby's own emotional state deteriorates because of the kept-inside pressure until he and his brother come to blows about what the drug use is doing to the family.

Of course teenage boys still enter relationships with girls; and young adult literature has progressed from the chaste dating Frank and Joe Hardy experienced during the 1950s. In *24 Girls in 7 Days* by Alex Bradley, Jack Grammar is shot down by his crush when he finally asks her to go to prom. The humiliating experience is magnified when his friends post an online personal ad asking girls to contact Jack because he needs a date. Hilariously funny, this book shows the doubts a teen male has about dating; and also shows teenage girls being somewhat aggressive in their pursuit of the nice-guy Jack.

From these few examples, you can see that authors writing young adult books for boys still include time-tested traits of guy novels such as doing the right thing, embarking on adventures, using technology, competing in sports, confronting the dangers of alcohol and drug use, and getting involved with girls. But on the other hand, today's books for guys are edgier and more realistic. They take themes that have long attracted boys to reading, tweak them, and make them even better.

Airborn by Kenneth Oppel

Babylon Boyz by Jess Mowry

The Black Book: Diary of a Teenage Stud by Jonah Black
   Vol. 1 *Girls, Girls, Girls*
   Vol. 2 *Stop, Don't Stop*
   Vol. 3 *Run, Jonah, Run*
   Vol. 4 *Faster, Faster, Faster*

Feed by M.T. Anderson

Midnighters #1: The Secret Hour by Scott Westerfeld

Mortal Engines (The Hungry City Chronicles) by Philip Reeve

Playing in Traffic by Gail Giles

Runner by Carl Deuker

Trouble Don't Last by Shelley Pearsall

Books for Guys Where the Male Characters Display Integrity

REFERENCES

Aronson, Marc. *Beyond the Pale: New Essays for a New Era*. Lanham, MD: Scarecrow Press, 2003.

The Book of Hit Singles Top 20 Charts from 1954 to Present Day. Compiled by Dave McAleer. San Francisco, CA: Backbeat Books, 2001.

Dresang, Eliza T. *Radical Change: Books for Youth in a Digital Age*. New York: H. W. Wilson, 1999.

Halls, Kelly Milner. "Oh Boy: Children's Author Compiles Anthology of Stories to Get Young Guys Excited about Reading." *The Denver Post* (May 1, 2005), F-09.

Meyer, Adam. *The Last Domino*. New York: G. P. Putnam's Sons, 2005.

Myers, Walter Dean. *Monster.* New York: HarperCollins, 1999.
Quick Picks for Reluctant Young Adult Readers Policies and Procedures, http://www.ala.org/ala/yalsa/booklistsawards/quickpicks/ quickpicksreluctantyoungadult.htm, accessed on February 21, 2007.
Scieszka, Jon. *Guys Write for Guys Read.* New York: Viking, 2005.
Sullivan, Michael. "Why Johnny Won't Read." *School Library Journal* (August 2004): 36.
Tyre, Peg. "The Trouble With Boys." *Newsweek* (January 30, 2006): 44–52.
Young Adult Library Services Association, http://www.ala.org/yalsa, accessed on March 10, 2005.

WORKS CITED

Bradley, Alex. *24 Girls in 7 Days.* New York: Dutton Books, 2005.
Colfer, Eoin. *Artemis Fowl.* New York: Hyperion, 2001.
———. *Artemis Fowl: The Arctic Incident.* New York: Hyperion, 2002.
———. *Artemis Fowl: The Eternity Code.* New York: Hyperion, 2004.
———. *Artemis Fowl: The Opal Deception.* New York: Hyperion, 2005.
Deuker, Carl. *High Heat.* Boston, MA: Houghton Mifflin, 2003.
Horowitz, Anthony. *Stormbreaker.* New York: Philomel, 2001.
———. *Point Blank.* New York. Philomel, 2001.
———. *Skeleton Key.* New York. Philomel, 2003.
———. *Eagle Strike.* New York. Philomel, 2003.
———. *Scorpia.* New York: Philomel, 2005.
———. *Ark Angel.* New York: Philomel, 2006.
McCormick, Patricia. *My Brother's Keeper.* New York: Hyperion, 2005.
McDonald, Janet. *Brother Hood.* New York: Farrar, Straus & Giroux, 2004.
McNamee, Graham. *Acceleration.* New York: Wendy Lamb Books, 2003.
Mikaelsen, Ben. *Touching Spirit Bear.* New York: HarperCollins, 2001.
Murray, Jaye. *Bottled Up.* New York: Dial, 2003.
Myers, Walter Dean. *Monster.* New York: HarperCollins, 1999.
Wallace, Rich. *Wrestling Sturbridge.* New York: Knopf, 1996.

Chapter 4

READING AND BOYS: TOPICS OF INTEREST

For years school librarians have conducted "library orientation" sessions, often directed to middle school students entering sixth grade. The purpose is simple. The teacher and librarian wish to familiarize the students with the school library's collection so they can more efficiently locate materials when they are given report assignments during the school year.

One of the basic concepts introduced to the students is that of the library housing two types of books, fiction and nonfiction. Often the sixth-graders being oriented are thrown off course by the one-question impromptu quiz, "Who can tell us the difference between fiction and nonfiction?" It always seems some poor kid gets confused which type of book comes from the author's imagination.

In the twenty-first century, the library orientation tour goes way beyond the simple breakdown of two types of books. Many librarians now point out proper use of computers for information retrieval, list the subscribed full-text databases available, and instruct the students on Internet search strategies using megasearch engines. However, even with technology firmly in place in most libraries, we can safely assume that school and public libraries providing service to teens continue to have a basic separation of nonfiction and fiction books. Another simple and basic assumption is that libraries serving teens are committed to including both fiction and nonfiction titles in their book collections. However, the two book categories may not receive equal consideration when it comes to readers.

BALANCE FICTION AND NONFICTION

In public libraries, particularly in young adult areas, you may have noticed, as I have, that there seems to be more fiction than nonfiction titles for teen readers. In contrast, school libraries and academic libraries seemingly tend to have more nonfiction books in their collections. As a librarian working with young adults, be aware of the population you serve and create a quality collection with the budget allotted. Make sure to balance your collection between male and female reading tastes and also between fiction and nonfiction titles. Nonfiction titles include recreational reading as well as volumes that enhance the local academic curriculum.

A longtime publisher and author of teen books, Marc Aronson, states that the number of young adult titles being published is on the rise, up to 23 percent from 1999. He further points out that more titles mean more changes to attract readers. He states, "... the very term YA has begun to splinter into sub-categories: fantasy (bringing boy readers into stores and libraries); graphic novels (a genre once only found in comic stores); funny, sexy, books with unreliable girl narrators (chick-lit); and rap-inspired poetry" (Aronson 2005).

Why this tremendous boom in teen books? The answer is simple. The teen population is currently growing, and it is projected that by 2010 it will have become the largest teen population ever. Aronson concludes, "... this proliferation of genres is that it increases the odds that more teenage readers will find something they will like ..." (Aronson 2005).

In addition to the increasing number of fiction books being published, the type of nonfiction titles available to teens is also on the rise. In his book, *Connecting Young Adults and Libraries*, Patrick Jones suggests that, "Part of being an adolescent is developing an intellectual curiosity and asking the question "Why?" (Jones 1998). Nonfiction speaks to that curiosity. Jones also offers an organizational list of nonfiction by providing categories listed as Recreational, Informational, Educational, and Reference (Jones 1998), adding that a library must reflect the priorities of its patrons, in this case young adults and the library.

Teachers tend to assign topics that are currently in the news; and teens need information on these topics to successfully construct reports. However, Jones commented on educational nonfiction books and their place in the library back in 1998, he was ahead of the curve when he stated, "With the proliferation of Internet access and full-text magazine services on the Internet and CD-ROM, seemingly fewer students are requiring these types of books" (Jones 1998).

In the young adult fiction world, plots and themes contained in the latest titles are overall edgier than was the case in years past, a trait that has caused controversy and concern among adults, from professionals to parents. For example, it is not uncommon for a young adult title to address issues of sex, drugs, or suicide—sometimes all within the same story. Some adults wish to limit titles available to teens by placing content labels on covers similar to movie ratings, or to eliminate certain titles from young adult library collections. Needless to say, decisions like these, if implemented, would certainly discourage boys from reading—at least from reading those titles labeled as appropriate for them.

WHAT DO GUYS LIKE TO READ?

How does all this relate to young adult male readers? And what are the implications for your library collection? Let's start with a simple observation: many boys prefer to read nonfiction books. But those nonfiction books are not necessarily informational, educational, or reference books; they are, instead, recreational nonfiction. That is, they are not necessarily books that are components of a formal learning curriculum.

The typical fiction collection at a public library (or bookstore) appeals to most adult patrons and possibly teenage girls; but how well does it appeal to teenage boys? Are there enough choices of what boys want to read, such as action-adventure or sports novels; or is the collection heavy on romance or problem novels featuring teen female characters? Recent professional articles have stressed the importance of reading for boys during their teenage years. Samplings of these readings are worth examining.

In an attempt to build support for boys while meeting their educational needs, First Lady Laura Bush commented in a *Newsweek* interview about the Helping America's Youth initiative, "... boys are more likely to be involved in gangs, they're more likely to end up in jail, they're more likely to commit crimes or to actually have crime committed against them."

Mrs. Bush also pointed out that boys seem to have the deck stacked against them by society's expectations. She continued, "I also think we've bought in, in our country, to the stereotype about boys that boys don't cry and boys should be totally self-reliant, that somehow they don't need the same nurturing and protection that girls get."

The First Lady then took these observations and applied them to the importance of reading. "The students who drop out usually are the ones who can't read or who are reading so far below their grade level that they are both frustrated and embarrassed to stay in school" (*Newsweek*, February 28, 2005).

Concern about boys and reading has been voiced by a person very close to the upper levels of American government. The question remains, how can boys be encouraged to become better and more active readers?

In the Foreword of his recently published story collection, *Guys Read*, author (and creator of the Web site http://www.guysread.com) Jon Scieszka states, "Hey guys—now here is something for you to read. A bunch of pieces by a bunch of guys ... all about being a guy" (Scieszka 2005). This book contains some outstanding writing by many of the top male authors for young adults, but the underlying message is "this is a title boys must read because there just isn't much else out there for them."

I disagree. There are, in fact, many titles out there for boys to read. Some are marked by great writing; and others simply have guy appeal, even though they will never make any top literary lists. As professionals, we all want to steer teens to "good books" ("good" meaning quality literature) but if a teenage male just wants to read a story that is full of action, but lacking in literary credentials, is that so bad?

Imagine for a moment a survey intended to target a range of adult professionals in the book or reading field. Imagine that this survey includes a question about the importance of turning young adults into lifelong readers and asks whether achieving that goal is an important part of their job. Overwhelmingly the response would be a positive one. However, as we have seen, sometimes through their actions and practices, educators and librarians inadvertently steer young adult males away from the ultimate goal of becoming lifelong readers.

In his article "Why Johnny Won't Read," in *School Library Journal*, Michael Sullivan states, "We define good books as those that conform to the way girls think. And when teachers assign students 'to read a book,' nonfiction books are often off-limits—according to some educators" (Sullivan 2004).

For years, nonfiction's role in young adult literature (and perhaps the main purpose of many entire young adult collections) has been to be a supplement to learning curriculums. Rows of titles, neatly arranged on library shelves by subject, patiently await the moment when a teen pulls the book as a potential information source for a report or research project. This traditional philosophy of nonfiction's role, relegates the books to being used only when a school assignment is nearing its deadline. Many teens, especially boys, pick up on this, and come to believe that the only reason to go to a library and select a book is to locate assignment resources. Reading for pleasure may not even occur to them.

CHANGES IN FORMAT

Publishers have begun to change their production and marketing strategies for nonfiction, and many librarians and educators have started to buy into the latest trend of acquiring "recreational nonfiction," or sometimes called "readable fiction," "nonfiction that reads like fiction," or "creative nonfiction."

Today, publishers produce nonfiction titles for teens in a wide variety of formats and on a wide variety of topics that are not necessarily linked to school reports. Flush with illustrations (usually color photographs), the information is broken up into sections, lists, timelines, captions under the photographs, and information boxes that enhance the topic.

Changes in the appearance of nonfiction have not happened overnight. In her book, *Radical Change: Books for Youth in a Digital Age*, Eliza T. Dresang examined the graphic format of books back in 1999. In her study, several key points are presented that define what makes a book referred to as graphic.

- Color is generously used to convey meaning. Specific colors make take the place of words.
- Pictures, maps, or graphs play a predominant part in a book that might be expected to have mostly words.
- Words represent sounds or transmit meaning by the way they are designed or placed on the page.
- A printed message is superimposed on a picture, appearing simultaneously as both words and picture.

What Makes a Nonfiction Book Graphic.
Source: Dresang, Eliza T. *Radical Change: Books for Youth in a Digital Age*. New York: H. W. Wilson, 1999, p. 82.

Today's teens are constantly bombarded visually—by television, by billboards and shopping malls, as well as by the dazzling visuals from the Internet coming through their home computer. In fact, television has had a huge influence over several preceding generations. Dresang informs us that, "Generation X, born between 1966 and 1977, grew up after television had become commonplace" (Dresang 1999).

Responding to this constant visual presence, books and book publishers adapted. In today's digital world, books use visual information in place of words and vice versa. What has evolved are books that vastly differ from those published just 10 to 15 years ago; and the visual images now enhancing books signify a huge shift in the format of books and how books are received by the public. Dresang even goes so far as to suggest that today's books have adopted concepts used by photo albums and scrapbooks, which seem friendly and approachable. Thus, the books combine the lure of the digital media with the comfort of a handheld book (Dresang, 1999).

Children and teens today are not disturbed by nonlinear narrative. Teens today can pick up a nonfiction book, open it to any page, begin reading, and they will be able to grasp the concept that is on that random page. No longer must eyes travel left to right in a repeated pattern, page after page. Instead, they can bounce from visual to caption to a list or an information box to quickly comprehend the information.

These highly visual books are what teen readers are accustomed to seeing and reading. Pictures within pictures, or television and information scrolls along the bottom of the screen (such as those on ESPN and CNN) are commonplace. In fact, the pop-up videos shown on MTV are based on the idea of eyes traveling around the screen and not fixed in one spot.

Teens are also completely in tune with their computer screens and often tile windows, keeping several open at a time to toggle back and forth, reading what comes onto the screen (the computer often changes the information every few seconds). It is not unusual to see teens online with several instant message windows open, along with a gaming Web site so they can check the latest versions of video games. The opening homepage of America Online has at least seven different links for information, and it entices the user with a photograph and a headline about the event. Framed by current weather statistics, the homepage lists links to even more information at the side of the screen. This is the busy nature (possibly viewed as cluttered or confusing to many adults) of teen reading in the online environment. After spending several hours surfing dazzling and colorful sites on the Internet, straight-line text just does not translate into something a teen is interested in. Publishers seem to be scrambling to catch up with this phenomenon, and in the past 8 to 10 years, nonfiction titles have become increasingly visual.

Quick 5	Ganz, Nicholas. *Graffiti World: Street Art from Five Continents*. New York: Harry N. Abrams, 2004. Illustrated with over 2,000 full-color photographs, this comprehensive book presents stunning examples of graffiti including subway art. Packard, Mary. *Ripley's Believe It or Not, Special Edition 2005*. New York: Scholastic, 2004. A glossy guide to the strange but true facts enhanced by outrageous photographs. Platt, Richard. *Crime Scene: The Ultimate Guide to Forensic Science*. New York: Dorling Kindersley, 2003. This title uses amazing digital imagery to show how science helps uncover the truth about crimes that were committed. Rohrer, Russ. *Ten Days in the Dirt: The Spectacle of Off-Road Motorcycling*. St. Paul, MN: Motorbooks International, 2004. Photographs will draw boys to the high-octane world of off-road motorcycling events including hill climbs and triple jumps. Schiff, Nancy Rica. *Odd Jobs: Portraits of Unusual Occupations*. Berkeley, CA: Ten Speed Press, 2002. From the cover photograph of an underarm deodorant tester performing her work, this is truly a book enhanced by the visuals.

Nonfiction Books for Guys That Are Visually Interesting

What does this trend mean for teenage male readers? Now they have books in a format that fits their reading needs. The topic (or more likely, the great cover art) will draw them to the book, and the visual layout inside further entices them into the subject. So, they begin to browse through the pages and read. This format change encourages teen males to read nonfiction and steers them to a wide variety of types of nonfiction books including biographies, how-to-do-it titles, and informational books about practically anything that will interest a boy reader.

BOOKS ARE BECOMING MORE VISUAL

Even fiction titles are beginning to incorporate visuals mixed in the story's text. For example, several sections of Walter Dean Myer's *Autobiography of My Dead Brother* are quite similar to a graphic novel and the illustrations add to the novel's flow.

It's quite likely that boys today read nonfiction more than ever before, but with these new visual books, that use is difficult to measure. These books are often are simply browsed, and then left on a library table, so no circulation figures are tallied. Here's where your observation skills and other measurements come into play. Instead of relying on circulation statistics, have your shelvers do some rough tallies of books that are reshelved into the stacks from library tables. Watch teens, and notice the types of materials they are browsing. Are they being browsed by individual readers, or by groups of boys, discussing and debating a book's content? Boys are curious about the world around them and want to learn more about it—nonfiction addresses that curiosity. Boys want to read about the sport superstars shown on the ESPN's Top 10 Plays of the Week. Lives of famous celebrities from movies, television, and music videos spark their curiosity and the more money the celebrity earns, the bigger the draw for readers (Oprah, Bill Gates, Eminem, 50 Cent, and Shaq—the list is endless).

All teens are bombarded by the media, which shoots sound bites and photo ops at them on a 24/7 basis. Boys (and perhaps girls too) often feel the urge to learn more about what they see. Thus librarians may witness boys reading about killer tsunamis, UFO sightings, volcanoes, NASCAR, and how to draw cartoon villains.

The drawbacks to this type of reading? Educators (and to an extent librarians) might not recognize this type of nonfiction as quality literature; and they may not consider the nonlinear type of reading it generates as legitimate reading. Since publishers have started making nonfiction appear like scrapbooks, photo albums, and magazines, educators don't see the information as in-depth. Also, the nonlinear format of today's nonfiction is foreign to adults who, for example, may consider an oversized book on the military's special forces just another picture book without much value, educational purpose, or quality.

When faced with these opinions or attitudes, consider the fact that a highly visual nonfiction work does not bog the reader down with extended paragraphs or pages attempting to describe an event or an item. The text is to the point, and the description is conveyed in the photograph for the reader to absorb. The information is actually complete, but appears in a more readable format. Today's nonfiction does not fit into a set formula, and the photographs and illustrations make each book unique unto itself. In the traditional nonfiction series that were published only 10 or 12 years ago, text-heavy design templates were used, so only the subject changed— the format stayed pretty much the same. With today's nonfiction, the use of color illustrations makes each book look fresh. Finally, good illustrations, color photographs, and visual graphics give readers a sense of time and place for the information presented. Comprehension of a subject becomes easier when readers feel they are a part of that world, and great graphic design accomplishes that.

While the information is accurate and essentially the same as presented in a nonfiction book that is strictly text, a highly visual nonfiction title will likely be used more by teens, and particularly male teens. Does this make of a higher quality? It's an arguable point, but today, many of the traditional, text-heavy nonfiction series sit on shelves as teens turn to the Internet for easier access to the information. Visual nonfiction bridges the Internet and traditional nonfiction.

It really boils down to this: Boys like to read about real things rather than abstract concept. They like to read about action. Whether their reading tastes are satisfied by a very visual nonfiction title or a page-turning suspense novel, the reading needs of boys must be taken into consideration. The next chapter will take you from knowing what types of books boys want to read to specific titles, genres, and subjects that are indeed boy-worthy.

REFERENCES

Aronson, Marc. "Getting over the Rainbow Party." *Publisher's Weekly* (August 15, 2005): 66.

Dresang, Eliza T. *Radical Change: Books for Youth in a Digital Age*. New York: H. W. Wilson, 1999.

Jones, Patrick. *Connecting Young Adults and Libraries*. 2nd ed. New York: Neal-Schuman, 1998.

"Laura, Sitting Pretty." *Newsweek* (February 28, 2005): 35.

Scieszka, Jon. *Guys Write for Guys Read*. New York: Viking, 2005.

Sullivan, Michael. "Why Johnny Won't Read." *School Library Journal* (August 2004): 36–39.

Chapter 5

BOOKS FOR BOYS—GENRES, TITLES, AND TOPICS

NONFICTION FOR TEEN MALES

In spite of the value of nonfiction, few, if any, of the traditional teaching aspects associated with fiction are linked to nonfiction. Educators do not look to nonfiction as books that provide character development or emotional conflicts; and the books often lack the resolution that a narrative story holds. Literary critics and scholars have for centuries focused on the attributes of fiction. Thus, recommending nonfiction reading takes educators out of their comfort zones, and away from teaching concepts associated with novels.

Award lists annually produced by YALSA (Young Adult Library Services Association of the American Library Association) are loaded with quality recommended fiction titles, while only a handful of nonfiction titles make the lists. Nonfiction can be found scattered through the Alex Awards, Best Books for Young Adults, but the committee that more readily considers nonfiction is Quick Picks for Reluctant Young Adult Readers. There you can find many of the highly visual, readable nonfiction titles that appeal to boys.

From the 2005 awards lists, 5 of the 10 Alex Award books are nonfiction. Of the Top 10 Best Books for Young Adults, only 1 of the 10 books is nonfiction; and from the complete list, 13 of 86 titles are nonfiction (one nonfiction title from the list is Walter Dean Myers' poetry anthology, *Here in Harlem: Poems in Many Voices*). On the Top 10 Quick Picks for Reluctant Young Adult Readers, 4 of the top 10 titles selected are nonfiction and 27 of the total 80 titles listed are nonfiction. For the 2006 awards list, 2 of the 10 Alex Award books are nonfiction. Of the Top 10 Best Books for Young Adults, 2 of the 10 titles are nonfiction, and from the complete list, 20 of the 91 titles are nonfiction. On the Top 10 Quick Picks for Reluctant Young Adult Readers, 3 of the Top 10 titles are nonfiction and 52 of the 105 titles (including all volumes of series selections) are nonfiction. The numbers continue in a similar pattern for 2007. Two of the 10 Alex Award books are nonfiction. Of the Top 10 Best Books for Young Adults, all 10 titles are fiction; and from the complete list, 14 of the 82 titles are nonfiction. On the Top 10 Quick Picks for Reluctant Young Adult Readers, 3 of the Top 10 titles are nonfiction and 29 of the 78 titles are nonfiction. Of course, graphic novels in some libraries are shelved by their Dewey designation and may be considered nonfiction (see http://www.ala.org/yalsa/booklistsawards/booklistsbook.htm).

Faced with these statistics, one might conclude that although nonfiction is recognized by award-winning committees, it is not given equal attention, appreciation, or support. That is bad news for boys who prefer reading nonfiction. The chances of their reading tastes being accepted is less than that of a fiction reader in the first place; and without official recognition or endorsements, finding quality nonfiction for them becomes more difficult.

One exception to the fiction-nonfiction imbalance can be found on the current lists devoted only to the recommendation and promotion of nonfiction titles in the journal, *VOYA* (Voice of Youth Advocates). Annually appearing in the August issue is the "Nonfiction Honor List." The selection criteria is brief, but the key point is that to gain a spot on the list, a book displays, "Unique research, creative presentation, inventive use of photography or illustrations, and filling a topic niche in the middle level . . . " (*VOYA* 2005).

Selections from the 2005 list include titles that may lure teenage boys, such as *The Tarantula Scientist* (Montgomery, Sy. Boston, MA: Houghton Mifflin, 2004), *Wild Science: Amazing Encounters between Animals and the People Who Study Them* (Miles, Victoria. Vancouver, BC: Raincoast Books, 2004), and *A Day that Changed America: Earthquake!* (Tanaka, Shelley. New York: Hyperion, 2004). *VOYA* has taken a progressive and timely lead to create this annual list, establishing credibility and acknowledging the change in nonfiction from crank-them-out series to vibrant and interesting titles that will entice teens.

Breaking away from the traditional Dewey categories for nonfiction, grouping the books by their interest and appeal can reveal a wide range of nonfiction titles that have young adult male interest. Let's take a closer look at how you can get nonfiction off the shelves and into the hands of male teen readers.

PROMOTING NONFICTION IN THE TEEN AREA

The Dewey Decimal and Library of Congress cataloging systems, long-time organizational tools for shelving nonfiction, have been used in standard procedures at libraries for decades; and they bring order to nonfiction collections. Without question these systems serve their necessary purpose of grouping nonfiction books on a particular topic in one area. For research purposes, this organization makes it easier for patrons to find materials without wasting hours searching all corners of the library. On the other hand, the use of these organizational systems and strict adherence to shelving books according to them limits the use of nonfiction. Unless they are displayed, the majority of these titles remain on the shelves until a patron, by use of the library's catalog, locates them for a given assignment or research project.

To promote readable nonfiction and support male teens in their reading interests, become more proactive with your nonfiction collection. Promote nonfiction titles with creative displays and place them in locations that automatically capture the attention of patrons.

Here are some tips on how to display nonfiction to enable teenage boys to more easily find the books that interest them, and increase circulation.

Display Titles Face-Out

Many teen areas have begun emulating the bookstore technique of showing the cover of the book on the shelves to attract patrons to the current "hot" titles. Covers of nonfiction books can be every bit as eye-catching as the covers of fiction, or even graphic novels or magazines. Take advantage of the alluring cover designs of your nonfiction titles to promote the collection simply by placing selected titles face-out on empty spots at the end of shelves, or on top of a lower bookcase where the book can be viewed at eye level.

You can take this technique a step further by weeding, and removing outdated nonfiction titles, thereby freeing up a shelf in the center of the nonfiction shelves. This middle shelf can then be used to prop up books and display their great covers; it will catch the eye of shelf browsers.

Although face-out display seems like a no-brainer, it is often forgotten with nonfiction books. Retail outlets ranging from bookstores and gift shops to grocery stores use this method to move inventory. You'll be surprised how many books your patrons actually pick up when they are displayed this way. Remember this very effective way to promote all of your titles.

Themed Displays

You have another opportunity to promote readable nonfiction by centering displays around pop culture themes that appeal to teens. This is a great way to connect with teenage boys. When selecting a theme, make a conscious attempt to include guy-friendly topics. Given below are topics that attract teenage guys to a nonfiction book display.

Music—Alternative, Hip-hop, Rap, and Heavy Metal

Not all young adult librarians have the responsibility of ordering music. This task in larger libraries is often controlled by an audiovisual or fine arts department. If you are one of the lucky ones that have control over order teen music, this is a great opportunity to combine formats in one display. Place selected music biographies in with titles about how to break into the recording industry, along with music recordings. If not already eliminated, many libraries are beginning to phase out cassette tapes. However CDs, selected from the latest new samples for a teen music collection, and sprinkled throughout the display would be a great draw for teens and will connect them in one step to reading material on the topic. To give an extra flourish to the display, include current magazines dealing with the music industry, such as *Vibe, XXL, Rolling Stone*, and *Revolver*.

Tattoos

It seems every celebrity from either movies or the sports world has a tattoo, and this is without a doubt a hot topic for teens. There are several great books about the culture surrounding tattoos, such as *Celebrity Skin: Tattoos, Brands and Body Adornments of the Stars* (Gerard, Jim. New York: Thunder's Mouth Press, 2001), *In the Paint: Tattoos of the NBA and the Stories Behind Them* (Gottlieb, Andrew. New York: Hyperion, 2003), and

Hot Bodies, Cool Styles: New Techniques in Self-Adornment (Polhemus, Ted. New York: Thames & Hudson, 2004).

Wars—Especially the War in Iraq

From the history of the conflicts to weapons and equipment used in battle to stories about the men overcoming hardships and horrors of war are sure guy draws. This display can include both fiction and nonfiction; and can also have news magazines such as *Time* and *Newsweek* mixed in with the books to further enhance the look of the display. These titles about twentieth-century warfare will catch guys' eyes. *10,000 Days of Thunder: A History of the Vietnam War* (Caputo, Philip. New York: Atheneum Books for Young Readers, 2005), *Fallen Angels* (Myers, Walter Dean. New York: Scholastic, 1988), *Search and Destroy* (Hughes, Dean. New York: Atheneum Books for Young Readers, 2005), *Inside Delta Force: The Story of America's Elite Counterterrorist Unit* (Haney, Eric. New York: Delacorte Press, 2006), and *The Last True Story I'll Ever Tell: An Accidental Soldier's Account of the War in Iraq* (Crawford, John. New York: Riverhead Books, 2005).

Cars and Car Repair

There are several coffee table-type books that feature customized rides and cars from practically any era, but what today's teens are interested in slick imports or muscle cars from the 1960s and 1970s. As two books for starting points, check out *Inside Monster Garage: The Builds, The Skills, The Thrills* (Vose, Ken. Des Moines, IA: Meredith Books, 2003), or *Monster Garage: How to Customize Damn Near Anything* (Klancher, Lee [ed.]. Osceola, WI: MBI, Sparkford, Haynes, 2003). The same teenage boys interested in these books will also likely be interested in customized chopper motorcycles. Although a little on the pricey side (around $30 per title), there are several oversized browsing books on this topic with great photographs.

Drawing Comics

Teenage boys are fascinated by the artwork presented in American comics, graphic novels, and manga-style books. Make a display mixing graphic novels and how-to-draw titles. Look for titles written by Christopher Hart that focus on specific aspects of design. Some examples are *Manga Mania Villains: How to Draw the Dastardly Characters of Japanese*

Comics (Hart, Christopher. New York: Watson-Guptill, 2003), and *Manga Mania Fantasy Worlds: How to Draw the Amazing Worlds of Japanese Comics* (Hart, Christopher. New York: Watson-Guptill, 2003). Again, spice up the display with magazines such as *NewType USA*, or *Shonen Jump*.

News Items Tie-Ins

Use the news as a springboard for a display. Following a tsunami, one library display highlighted disasters and books on natural disasters such as floods, volcanoes, earthquakes, hurricanes, and so on. Teens are aware of these major events, and are often curious to learn more, but may not know where to look, or have the confidence to ask a librarian.

Of course, you don't have to limit yourself to major events. This tidbit appeared in *The Week* magazine on August 12, 2002:

> *Of the 2,228 passengers who were aboard the RMS Titanic when it went down in 1912, three remain alive.*

From this item, a display of the many titles about the Titanic can be put together. Perhaps the display can be expanded to include other man-made disasters to contrast a display about natural disasters.

Another tidbit appeared in Cleveland's newspaper, *The Plain Dealer*, on May 30, 2005 on Memorial Day weekend:

> *Of the 4.7 million American servicemen who took part in World War I, only thirty remain alive.*

This item can lead to a display about World War I or all wars and it also provides a chance to display fictional titles about male teens in war such as *Private Peaceful* (Morpurgo, Michael. New York: Scholastic Press, 2004), *B for Buster* (Lawrence, Iain. New York: Delacorte Press, 2004), and *Soldier Boys* (Hughes, Dean. New York: Simon & Schuster, 2001).

With displays, you can mix fiction with nonfiction, genres with other genres, and formats with other formats (books, DVDs, CDs, and magazines). A passive display on a current news topic is a great way to promote your library's collection and satisfy teen curiosity.

The Weird

Guys are fascinated by the strange, the bizarre, and, yes, even the gross. Visual books such as *The Guinness Book of World Records*, *Ripley's Believe*

It or Not, Scholastic Book of World Records, and titles dealing with Urban Legends make great choices for displays. These are great browsing books and each title has many spin-offs that narrow down the weirdness even further. Enhance the display with a sign of a typed and enlarged factoid displayed near the titles.

To summarize, including nonfiction in your displays gives you a simple but very effective way to attract teenage males to all books. This is particularly true for visual or "readable" nonfiction titles. When creating your next display, don't forget this boy bait.

HOW-TO BOOKS: MUST-HAVE FOR GUYS

As previously stated, boys often feel the urge to do things, to build and create with their hands. Make sure your young adult nonfiction section includes a variety of how-to books, such as how to draw cartoons, how to learn martial arts, how to stylize a muscle car, or how to duplicate street-ball basketball moves. How-to books are great choices for male readers because they enable the young men to take information from the book's pages and apply it to something they want to do.

How-to books present information in a straightforward manner. They usually open with a brief overview providing background history, famous people who invented or were involved in the activity and current trends of the activity's evolvement.

After this initial overview, most of a how-to book informs the reader step-by-step instruction on the activity. Usually, instructions are accompanied by photographs or illustrations that guide the reader along the way. Some of the most popular how-to books at our library have a series of stop action photographs explaining key points of the activity. Of course, teenaged boys are more attracted to color photographs and that will enhance the appeal of any book.

Teen males are drawn to these books because the subject matter is often a reversal of school textbooks. How-to books not only teach skills that interest boys, but they can also see immediate results, something they cannot project from reading school curriculum support books. And finally, apart from the cut-and-dry format of instructional books, such as car repair manuals, how-to books provide a beginning, a middle, and an end to the activity—something that will appeal to boys' need of undertaking a task and completing it.

<table>
<tr><td rowspan="5"><h1>Quick
5</h1></td><td>And 1 and Palmer, Chris. Streetball: All the Ballers, Moves, Slams and Shine. New York: HarperResource, 2004.
    The stop action photos provide details on how to perform the slick basketball moves seen on ESPN2.</td></tr>
</table>

Quick 5	And 1 and Palmer, Chris. *Streetball: All the Ballers, Moves, Slams and Shine.* New York: HarperResource, 2004.
	    The stop action photos provide details on how to perform the slick basketball moves seen on ESPN2.
	
	Carton, Sean. *2005 Gamer's Almanac: Your Daily Dose of Tricks, Cheats and Fascinating Facts.* Indianapolis, IN: Que, 2004.
	    A one stop shopping source enabling readers to discover how to dominate the latest electronic games.
	
	Christensen, Loren. *Solo Training: The Martial Artist's Guide to Training Alone.* Hartford, CT: Turtle Press, 2001.
	    A tutorial informing readers how to adjust their training efforts to meet their individual needs.
	
	Davidson, Steve. *The Complete Guide to Paintball.* Long Island City, NY: Hatherleigh Press, 2004.
	    All the equipment, tactics, and strategies are outlined in this source about the growing sport of paintball.
	
	Hart, Christopher. *Manhwa Mania: How to Draw Korean Comics.* New York: Watson-Guptill, 2004.
	    Japanese manga and anime fans will discover what makes Korean comics unique.

How-To Books

BIOGRAPHY: BETTER ALIVE THAN DEAD

Biography can be a tough sell for teenage boys, because often their first experience with this type of literature comes through school, and usually in the form of a book report assignment. Educators, feeling compelled to recommend books that teach something, offer suggestions of books on famous figures (or types of famous people) who have limited appeal to today's teen males. Scientists from the Renaissance, classical music composers and explorers from the 1500s do not spark interest to today's teen readers. Often the students' choices come from a list of books found in the school library that were originally purchased to simply support a particular teacher's interest subject area. In addition, these suggested titles often are decades old. Today's teens do not recognize these people, and are disinterested about any possible contributions to history. As a public librarian, I have fielded teen requests for biography selections about famous mathematicians, Hispanic artists, and inventors from the nineteenth century. Other specific name requests for biographies have been scientist Madam Curie, president Abraham Lincoln, and explorer Marco Polo. Although the class may be studying these topics, these figures from history just do not pique interest. Teens will merely go through the motions of filling-in-the-blanks and hand in a formulated report.

Teens and teenage boys read and enjoy biography, but under their own set of rules or stipulations. First, the chances of attracting teenage male readers to a biography are greater if the famous person is still alive. Secondly, the subject should have a "rough-around-the-edges" quality—perhaps even been involved in a public scandal. Third, the person should be connected in some way to pop culture, someone who is seen on the electronic media. Unfortunately, these criteria are often not met with school assignments.

Let's take the issue a step further. Exactly what kinds of biographies do teenage boys like to read? Good question. Two categories that come to mind are contemporary sports and music. Boys like reading about sports figures, but a key factor has to be that the athlete is currently playing the sport. As soon as an athlete retires and falls off of the ESPN radar, teenage boys will likely lose interest in that person. A few years ago, librarians could not keep enough titles about sports star Michael Jordan on their shelves. Now that he's retired, his popularity has faded—at least as far as teen requests for biographies about him. Boys also enjoy biographies that give emphasis to the developmental years of the athlete rather than a bland listing of the athlete's statistics. And finally, photographs of the athlete build interest in the story, although they are not the key criteria for sports biographies.

When building your sports biography collection, avoid short formulated books that contain less than 50 pages on a single superstar, and instead acquire collected biographies with 3 or 4 pages for each athlete. These collected biographies often feature over 20 sports personalities in one volume. You'll get more bang for your buck, and the teens are more likely to browse and read the profiles in the collections.

With the Internet, cable television, and video games dominating their lives, teenage boys are more in tune with sports personalities participating in competitions beyond the traditional team sports (i.e., football, basketball, and baseball). For example, many male teens are currently interested in individual sports known as extreme sports, including skateboarding, motocross, BMX, and all the Gravity Games' sports. The Gravity Games now has three different competitions, Summer, Winter, and H_2O. Emphasizing freestyle events, competitions are constantly added with complete information located at http://www.gravitygames.com. Your library's nonfiction shelves can reflect this interest shift in sports information that especially appeals to teenage male readers.

Quick 5	Coyle, Daniel. *Lance Armstrong's War: One Man's Battle Against Fate, Fame, Love, Death, Scandal and a Few Other Rivals on the Road to the Tour de France.* New York: HarperCollins, 2005.
	    An inside look at the man striving to achieve what no other bicyclist has ever done.
	
	Hawk, Tony. *Hawk: Occupation, Skateboarder.* New York: ReganBooks, 2000.
	    Tony Hawk is the legend and benchmark that all skaters judge themselves.
	
	McGrath, Jeremy. *Wide Open: A Life in Supercross.* New York: HarperEntertainment, 2004.
	    It takes a special combination of talent and guts to excel, and McGrath has both.
	
	Morgan, Jr., David Lee. *LeBron James: The Rise of a Star.* Cleveland, OH. Gray & Co., 2003.
	    LeBron dominates sports' highlights but this biography reveals his humble childhood.
	
	Platt, Larry. *Only the Strong Survive: The Odyssey of Allen Iverson.* New York: ReganBooks, 2002.
	    An examination of Iverson's early background and career settle questions about the player known in the NBA as "The Answer."

Individual Sports Biographies

Quick 5	Gottlieb, Andrew. *In the Paint: Tattoos of the NBA and the Stories Behind Them.* New York: Hyperion, 2003.
	    Who has the most? What do they mean? And why did they get them? A fascinating look at NBA players who are covered with tattoos.
	
	Hareas, John. *NBA's Greatest.* New York: Dorling Kindersley, 2003.
	    This title features great photographs of past and present stars of the NBA.
	
	Leiker, Ken. *Unscripted.* New York: Pocket Books, 2003.
	    A behind-the-scenes look at what it is like to be a World Wrestling Entertainment superstar.
	
	Miller, Timothy and Milton, Steve. *NASCAR Now.* Buffalo, NY: Firefly Books, 2004.
	    This guide to NASCAR provides profiles of famous drivers and details of top racetracks.
	
	Tomlinson, Joe. *Extreme Sports: In Search of the Ultimate Thrill.* Richmond Hill, Ontario: Firefly Books, 2004.
	    Action photos show extreme sport athletes in performance and the book explains the sports' philosophy, techniques, and equipment.

Collected Sports Biographies

MUSIC: HIT ALL THE STOPS ON THE TOUR

Teens are bombarded by the rapidly changing music industry as various artists maneuver to hit the charts. All teens want to read about the musicians behind the music; but unfortunately, the staying power of many top bands and musicians is so fleeting that the group fades in popularity before any print biography can be written. However, while teenage boys tend to lose interest in sports celebrities after the star stops playing, they are seemingly more forgiving about musicians. Boys often read about musicians and music groups long after they fade from popularity. There is also the special allure of musicians who die young and become somewhat immortal in the eyes of the teenage fans. These deaths can be from decades ago, such as the death of Jimi Hendrix, to the 1990s suicide of Kurt Cobain. It is as if the music and the artist are both frozen in time, and the work of the deceased performer continues to appeal to teenage boys (and girls). In addition, retro is cool. (Another interesting observation I've made is that teenage boys often read about female musicians but seem to steer away from books about other female professionals such as sports stars or film actresses.)

Biography about musicians appeals to teenage boys and crosses all types of music types, from heavy metal, to alternative/rock, to hip-hop. Like sport biographies, music biographies are more readily read by boys if the book features a wide range of artists in a collected biographical format. Because teens' tastes in music vary widely in any community, be sure your library's nonfiction collection features samplings from as many different types of musical biographies as the budget allows. Keep in mind that these types of books about pop music and musicians do not support school curricula. Nonetheless, they are packed with information and are read by teenaged boys.

Quick 5	Cobain, Kurt. *Journals.* New York: Riverhead Books, 2002.
	Included in this title are thoughts, lyrics, drawings, and letters that filled Nirvana singer-songwriter Kurt Cobain's notebooks.
	Coker, Cheo Hodari. *Unbelievable: The Life, Death and Afterlife of the Notorious B.I.G.* New York: Three Rivers Press, 2003.
	This is the story that rocked the world, the larger-than-life Christopher Wallace, a.k.a. Biggie Smalls, a.k.a. The Notorious B.I.G.
	Grandberry, Omari. *O.* New York: MTV Books, 2005.
	Omarion chronicles his Los Angeles childhood, how B2K came together, and the ups and downs of instant brotherhood.
	Keys, Alicia. *Tears for Water: Songbook of Poems and Lyrics.* New York: G. P. Putnam's, 2004.
	Featuring the complete lyrics of Alicia Keys. Boys will read this book, using the words to impress girls.
	White, Armond. *Rebel for the Hell of It: The Life of Tupac Shakur.* New York: Thunder's Mouth Press, 1997.
	Discusses the personal, political, sociological, and musical forces that brought Tupac Shakur his fame, and his death.

Books about or Biographies of Individual Musicians

Quick 5	Baltin, Steve. *From the Inside: Linkin Park's Meteora.* Agoura Hills, CA: Bradson Press, 2004.
	This book gives fans a more intimate view of what the *Meteora* touring cycle looked like.
	Chirazi, Steffan. *So What? The Good, the Mad and the Ugly: The Official Metallica Illustrated Chronicles.* New York: Broadway Books, 2004.
	Outlined in this book is why Metallica has earned its reputation as one of the most highly regarded and hard-rocking bands of all time.
	Hip-Hop Divas. New York: Three Rivers Press, 2001.
	Teenage males will be interested in this collection of essays and photographs that profile the most influential female hip-hop artists.
	Light, Alan. *The Vibe History of Hip Hop.* New York: Three Rivers Press, 1999.
	Chronicles the history of hip-hop music from its origins on Brooklyn streets to its explosion as an international phenomenon.
	Kool Moe Dee. *There's a God on the Mic: The True 50 Greatest MCs.* New York: Thunder's Mouth Press, 2003.
	Passionate discussions among teenage males will arise from reading this list of the "50 Greatest."

Books about Musical Groups

MILITARY BOOKS: ACTION SPEAKS LOUDER THAN WORDS

The military and books about the military, both in fiction and nonfiction, have always held a special allure for males both adult and teen. The action found in military books offers many intangibles that appeal to teenage boys discovering their own personalities. Depending on your buddies, accomplishing tasks that are more important than your own interests and placing honor before self and accomplishing goals as a team, are all great guy themes and have traditionally drawn boys to reading. Today's nonfiction military books also often feature illustrations or photographs of a wide variety of weapons and technology used in war, visual items that are guy magnets. Due to the violent nature of war and the grim results of wounds and death, keep in mind that these types of books may be better suited for the older end of young adult male readers.

Quick 5	Bowden, Mark. *Black Hawk Down: A Story of Modern War.* New York: Atlantic Monthly Press, 1999. A classic in military literature, this book chronicles the breakdown of young soldiers caught in a violent firefight in Somalia. McManners, Hugh. *Ultimate Special Forces.* New York: Dorling Kindersley, 2003. Packed with photographs this book presents a vivid introduction to elite military units of Europe, Russia, Israel, and the United States. Melton, H. Keith. *Ultimate Spy.* New York: Dorling Kindersley, 1996. Descriptions and photographs of the ingenious tools and weapons used by intelligence agents around the world throughout history are provided. Nelson, Peter. *Left For Dead: A Young Man's Search for Justice for the USS Indianapolis.* New York: Delacorte, 2002. A student publishes the truth of the gripping account of the sinking of the USS Indianapolis at the end of World War II and subsequent captain's trial. Wright, Evan. *Generation Kill: Devil Dogs, Iceman, Captain America and the New Face of American War.* New York: G. P. Putnam's, 2004. Today's soldiers in Iraq, many as young as 19 are driven to endure the hazards and conditions of modern desert warfare.

Military Nonfiction Titles

THE MORE ACTION THE BETTER

One of the main reasons for the draw that nonfiction has to teenage males is that these titles often feature action, or encourage the reader to accomplish an act. Upon opening a great nonfiction title, the reader can immediately see that a person (not an imaginary character) is doing something and doing something using his body. This type of reading satisfies urges inside many developing teenage boys; the desire to accomplish a task and have a concrete result at the conclusion of the task. Of course instructional manuals inform a reader how to begin and finish tasks, but teenage males also enjoy nonfiction books that show action while providing instruction.

| Quick 5 | Capuzzo, Michael. *Close to Shore: The Terrifying Shark Attacks of 1916.* New York: Crown, 2003

During the summer of 1916 when swimming in the ocean became popular, three men and one boy were killed by the gruesome work of a rogue white shark.

Clarkson, Mark. *Battlebots: The Official Guide.* New York: McGraw-Hill/Osborne, 2002.

Combines engineering ability, mechanical parts, excess testosterone all in a duel to the death between machines.

Coombs, Davey. *MX: The Way of the Motocrosser.* New York: H.N. Abrams, 2003.

During a race motocross riders perform double- and triple-jumps and dodge tabletops, hills, rocks, mud, dust, and anything else that Mother Nature can throw at them.

Davis, James. *Skateboarding is Not a Crime: 50 Years of Street Culture.* Buffalo, NY: Firefly Books, 2004.

This title celebrates the sport and subculture of skateboarding and, by the way, 1 in 10 U.S. teenagers owns or rides a skateboard.

Klancher, Lee. *Monster Garage: How to Customize Damn Near Everything.* St. Paul, MN: Motorbooks International, 2003.

Jesse James asked the experts used on the number one Discovery Channel show, Monster Garage, and they provided a guide to customizing your car, motorcycle, minivan, pickup truck, toaster, . . . |

Nonfiction Books with Action

SUMMARY

The current trend of public libraries stocking their young adult non-fiction shelves with readable nonfiction and steering away from books on school curriculum topics is a movement that will attract teenage male readers. Budget cuts may limit the number of titles that may be acquired, but librarians working with teenage males and wishing to draw them into the library should definitely explore the idea of giving their nonfiction shelves a makeover and break away from acquiring only items that are used for classroom reports.

FICTION FOR TEEN MALES

Fiction is, of course, divided into different genres. Both adult and young adult readers appreciate the organizational techniques of bookstores and libraries that either section off types of books or label them with stickers signifying the book's content. There is not a genre called "guy books." In contrast, many publications, libraries, and bookstores promote "chick lit." Due to the phrase being somewhat sexist, it is not recommended to display books know as "chick lit" in a teen area with a sign stating it as such. All librarians (and booksellers) know of this subgenre and push patrons to it. Sometimes a kinder phrase such as "fiction for girls" can be used as a bibliography heading. You may wish to push "guy books" with a display stating that these titles have high "guy-appeal."

Teen males read books from all the traditional genres if the content appeals to their tastes in general. It does not matter if the book's category is science fiction, fantasy, mystery, or suspense. As long as the story moves, and is more plot-driven rather than character driven, chances are teen males will be receptive to selecting that title.

THE TEEN PROBLEM NOVEL—IT'S NOT A GUY THING

Any professional librarian, educator, or adult who works with teens may frequently find themselves browsing a public library's young adult collection or scanning a posted recommended reading list for teens. What often immediately stands out to these adults (who are familiar with the teenage mind) is that many of the titles available and suggested to teens are what are known as "problem novels." (Interestingly, when I browse the young adult sections of national chain retail bookstores, I seem to find that the titles prominently displayed were the less serious, light reading "chick-lit" or intricate and lengthy fantasy novels.)

Focusing on social or personal problems that teens may face while growing up, problem novels construct a plot around that problem. A teen character must then deal with the consequences of being involved in that serious issue. For example, problem novels might focus on drug and alcohol use and abuse, physical abuse from an adult or another teen, sexual abuse from an adult or another teen, date rape, sexual promiscuity, and teen pregnancy.

Problem novels, often described as being full of teen angst, are only a part of the wide range of young adult fiction available today. But these are often the titles that are promoted by public librarians and educators; and many have stood the test of time. To this day, one of the pioneering young adult problem novels from the 1960s, *The Outsiders* by S. E. Hinton, is a treasured book, dissected in classes by students, with tests on the meaning of the book given by countless English teachers. While *The Outsiders* has a certain amount of guy appeal, many problem novels feature female narrators or main characters. Book professionals who work with teens agree that teen fiction readers are most likely to be girls. Publishers and authors also are aware of that they have a greater chance of selling books if they target their products to teenage female readers; and character-driven books that are heavy with deep emotions appeal to teenage girls. Thus, problem novels have a powerful presence in young adult literature.

The problem with problem novels is exactly what draws female readers to them—they are layered thick with emotions that leave male readers behind. The average problem novel is not likely to appeal to or hold a guy's interest.

Laura Miller addresses this promotion of the teen problem novel in her essay that appeared in the *New York Times* titled, "A Good Book Should Make You Cry." In the essay, Miller relates the experiences of Barbara Feinberg, author of *Welcome to the Lizard Motel: Children, Stories, and the Mystery of Making Things Up,* and her 12-year-old son who loves to read. As a parent, Feinberg became curious about the genre of young adult problem novels. During a visit to her son's school and the school's library, she found books describing " . . . with spare realism, child and teenage protagonists weathering abuse, addiction, parental abandonment or fecklessness, mental illness, pregnancy, suicide, violence, prostitution or self-mutilation—and often a combination of the above." "Teachers love them," the local librarian explains as Feinberg scans a shelf of such titles. "They win all the awards."

But Alex Feinberg, the 12-year-old son being asked to read these problem novels, got directly to the typical reaction of a teen male reader to problem novels. "We can't ever say we don't like the books," Alex told his mother, because according to his teacher, "if you're not liking the books, you're not reading them closely enough." The books are so depressing—"'Everybody dies in them,' he [Alex] told me wearily" (Miller 2004). I cannot imagine many boys who after finishing a book, look forward to settling down for a three-Kleenex sob.

In response to the theory that top book award committees (Michael L. Printz, Newbery) and educators place a high value on problem novels. Daniel Handler, author of the best-selling Lemony Snicket series states there is a "wrong-headed belief that the more misery there is, the more quality there is, that the most lurid, unvarnished stories are closest to the truth" (Miller 2004).

So, there it is. There's a prevailing awareness throughout the professional book community that boys don't read or don't read enough, they don't like to read and are in danger of failing intellectually because of their avoidance of reading. But at the same time, educators and library professionals continue to promote problem novels, which generally have little appeal to guys.

That is not to say that all problem novels have zero appeal to guys. It is entirely possible that teenage males will be very interested in Zoe's determination to live apart from her alcoholic mother and overbearing grandmother by renting a room by herself, the basis of Mary E. Pearson's book *A Room on Lorelei Street* (Pearson, Mary E. New York: Henry Holt, 2005.) Desperate for cash, Zoe makes a deal with an adult to have him pay her for sex, a stunning scene that further pushes the envelope of young adult problem novels.

In John Green's excellent novel, *Looking for Alaska* (Green, John. New York: Dutton, 2005) (awarded the 2006 Michael L. Printz award), male characters attempt to understand why their beloved female classmate, Alaska Young, is tragically killed in a car crash when she was behind the wheel, driving drunk. The voices of the characters full of wit and sarcasm have guy appeal, but again, the tragedy is followed by many pages of characters emotionally trying to come to terms with Alaska's death, which could easily turn off the average teenage male reader.

A Room on Lorelei Street and *Looking for Alaska* are examples of well written teen novels, but middle-of-the-road teen male readers are not be drawn to them because the emphasis of the book is on the emotions of the characters, either voicing their feeling in dialogue or internally examining how they feel.

In recent years, however, problem novels have begun to merge with other genres or subgenres, increasing their level of guy appeal. Rare is the pure sport story where the majority of the book takes place on the field or court. Today's sports books take the reader away from the athletic action and place him or her into the problems the main character is challenged with away from the competition. There are many suspense novels in which the characters experience a certain level of angst or must overcome an emotional situation along with the main suspense of the plot. Do guys read problem novels? Yes, but it's more likely if the book is laced with action, the characters are doing something physical, and meet their problems head on, not just mentally pondering their inner emotions.

Quick 5	de la Pena, Matt. *Ball Don't Lie*. New York: Delacorte, 2005. Realistic teen fiction doesn't come any grittier than "Sticky's" problems as he lives to play pickup basketball at the Lincoln Rec Center in urban L. A.
	McCormick, Patricia. *My Brother's Keeper*. New York: Hyperion, 2005. Middle son Toby, age 13, struggles to keep his family together following his father's departure and takes extreme care to cover up his idolized older brother's drinking and drug use.
	McNamee, Graham. *Acceleration*. New York: Wendy Lamb, 2003. Duncan feels he must overcome his inner turmoil about a past accidental death and bravely begins to track down a serial killer in Toronto's underground subway system.
	Volponi, Paul. *Black and White*. New York: Viking, 2005. High school basketball stars Marcus and Eddie, a.k.a. Black and White, make the horribly wrong decision to use a pistol in armed robbery holdups and one of them will end up in jail.
	Wallace, Rich. *Wrestling Sturbridge*. New York: Knopf, 1997. Senior wrestler Ben comes to realize that the only way he can crack the starting lineup is to rat out Sturbridge's star wrestler, an athlete who breaks training rules by binge drinking.

Problem Novels That Appeal to Guys

FANTASY BOOKS—BEYOND *THE LORD OF THE RINGS*

Problem novels thick with introspective examinations of the characters and only minor scenes that involve action may steer boys away. On the other hand, fantasy novels have seemingly always had a loyal following of teenage male readers, and now with the Harry Potter phenomenon and Tolkien's *Lord of the Rings* trilogy having successful movie adaptations, fantasy is a great draw for both male and female teen readers. But does fantasy really have a widespread appeal for boys?

Adults working with teens often perceive fantasy as being too weighty, too highbrow and packed with lengthy descriptive wordings to have male appeal; and as a genre more suited to female teen readers. That is a good point, which can also be stated about any literary genre. But some characteristics of the genre draw teenage males. What are those characteristics? Before we answer that question, let's ground ourselves by defining the genre.

In the Webster's *Third New International Dictionary of the English Language*, fantasy fiction is defined as: "Imaginative fiction dependent for effect on strangeness of setting (as other worlds or times) and of characters (as supernatural or unnatural beings)" (Webster's, 1986).

Expanding on the Webster definition, Diana Tixier Herald, in her book, *Teen Genreflecting: A Guide to Reading Interests*, states that "Fantasy literature leads readers into realms of imagination and magic of inexplicable occurrences that don't have a solid foundation in reality as we know it" (Herald 2003).

So, is fantasy a genre that appeals to boys? Yes and no. Many boy readers are drawn to fantasy, and prefer it to problem novels, historical fiction, or sports stories. Other teen males have problems getting into a lengthy fantasy novel.

In fantasy novels, the pacing may be slow, especially in the early part of the story— or first book of a series—where the author has to set the cast of characters and also introduce the reader to the imaginary setting. Laying the groundwork for a story set in another universe (a parallel world, a town, kingdom, or region), where magic is the most important characteristic, takes time. This pulls the narrative away from any hint of action that might have attracted boy readers to the book in the first place. They may set the book aside after reading less than 20 pages, saying, "nothing happens in this book."

Boys, more often than girls, are likely to fall into the category of reluctant readers. A story must grab a reader in the first few pages to entice the reluctant reader to read more. Fantasy novels that take many pages to get to the action are very hard sells for reluctant readers. But that is not to say all fantasy has limited boy appeal.

Why Fantasy May Attract Teen Male Readers

Reading has long been acknowledged as an escape from everyday life. Teen males are no different than other readers, and at times they like to imagine themselves placed in a different environment. Fantasy accomplishes this task. Guys who read fantasy, read many, many, titles and seemingly cannot get enough of the genre. Of course there are elements of fantasy that have definite guy-appeal. Let's take a look at what fantasy characteristics bring boys to the books and keeps them coming back for more.

Beasts

Fantasy often features dragons, goblins, shape shifters, trolls, unicorns, serpents, or hybrid beasts, such as the Hippogriff (with the head and forelegs of an eagle and the body of a horse) found in the Harry Potter books. Beasts in fantasy tales may be powerful and dangerous, guard a special treasure the hero of the story seeks, or be incredibly violent. Whatever the author's purpose of the beast to the story—they often initially appear frightening, but are actually noble, and in fact are there to protect the protagonist. The power and potential danger a beast brings to a story is of great appeal to boys.

Magic

Well, of course there is magic in fantasy. Everyone knows that. But many fantasy titles feature a father-figure sorcerer who is somewhat world-weary but can still call upon his command of magic to destroy evil. Perhaps this is why the characters of Merlin and Gandalf have long attracted teen males to the Arthurian and Lord of the Rings adventures. It may be that boys are attracted to the control aspect of being able, at the flick of a wrist, to change the outcome of a battle or neutralize an opponent. Think of the allure of video games for boys, it is often all about power and control through the keyboard, joystick, or game controller.

Good versus Evil

Whether the characters rely on magic or not, often they are pitted against a large evil empire and either with a band of underdog outcasts or alone take on the task of challenging the evil. This is one of the reasons the *Star Wars* movies and literature has been such a huge draw over the years. In books, the concept of a lone, noble teen challenging a larger evil is a characteristic of Bobby Pendragon in D. J. MacHale's epic Pendragon series, a series with very high guy-appeal.

Heroes

The epic hero has always been a draw for boy readers, dating back to the *Odyssey* and Beowulf; and both of these enduring heroes' stories are required reading in high school literature classes. Epic heroes are noble, courageous, self-sacrificing, loyal, and oftentimes male—flawed or incomplete, yet powerful. They frequently embark on seemingly impossible quests to save others. What's not to like if you are a teenage boy trying to figure out what it takes to become a man?

Danger, Violence, and Battles

After reading many pages of a fantasy novel, readers are often treated to the climatic battle scenes. Here, characters prove their mettle while several peripheral characters and evildoers meet their deaths. Boy readers may tolerate lengthy character development or relationship problems between the characters if they can be assured of great battle scenes that bring in good versus evil. Tolkien's *Lord of the Rings* trilogy and also his book *The Hobbit* are perfect examples of fantasy stories that result in a climatic test of the characters' courage in battle.

So, some fantasy novels appeal to boys, and others don't. In order to appeal to boys, a fantasy has to have the boy-tested characteristics listed above. For example, some boy readers are interested in reading stories about the character of Merlin. Most boys would rather read the T. A. Barron's more guy-friendly and adventurous *The Lost Years of Merlin* series rather than the longer in length book, *The Crystal Cave* by Mary Stewart, which is heavy with character development. Both deal with the Arthurian legend and Merlin, but Barron's books have more guy-appeal.

A recent trend in young adult literature is the blend of fantasy with other types of books. Consider these blended types of fantasy. By taking elements from humorous stories or traditional adventure books, two recent fantasy series that have guy appeal are the *A Series of Unfortunate Events* books by Lemony Snicket and the Artemis Fowl series by Eoin Colfer.

Any discussion of fantasy cannot ignore the fabulously successful Harry Potter series by J. K. Rowling. These titles, of course, are hugely popular. Although they are lengthy books, they have broad appeal to guys—from the creepy happenings in the depths of Hogwarts, to Harry relying on his uncovered wizardry skills to rescue his friends.

Rowling has masterfully incorporated many guy elements in this series, a lone individual battling a strong evil being, loyalty to friends, courage in the face of danger and death. However, a word of caution—the sixth book in the series steers more to relationships with less thrilling action than previous titles, possibly making the *Harry Potter and the Half-Blood Prince* (Rowling, J. K. New York: Arthur Levine Books, 2005) more appealing to girls and less to boys. Perhaps this is a setup for the final episode to this wonderful series that has launched a new generation of readers, including teen male readers. I certainly hope that Harry continues to draw boys into reading.

As an aside note, the dreaded reader's advisory question from teens directed at a teen librarian is: "Do you have any books like Harry Potter?" Here are three titles to keep in mind: *The Amulet of Samarkand: The Bartimaeus Trilogy,* Book 1 (Stroud, Jonathan. New York: Hyperion, 2003). The second book in the series, *The Golem's Eye* (Stroud, Jonathan. New York: Hyperion, 2004) features Nathaniel who summons up the *djinni* Bartimaeus and instructs him to battle powerful and magical beings. The third book in the series, *Ptolemy's Gate* (Stroud, Jonathan. New York: Hyperion, 2006), has recently been released; and a drop-off in popularity of the series is not anticipated. Another title to suggest to Harry Potter fans is *Percy Jackson and the Olympians: The Lightning Thief* (Riordan, Rick. New York: Miramax Books, 2005) where Percy comes to understand he is the son of Poseidon and is given the charge to steal back Zeus' favorite lightning bolt from Hades. The second book in the series, *The Sea of Monsters* (Riordan, Rick. New York: Miramax Books, 2006.), released in the spring of 2006, has the luxury of not dragging readers through pages of story set up. The action starts early, is fast and furious, and only stops at the very last page.

While fantasy may not always meet the broad set of characteristics that boys require, it is a genre with boy appeal. There are dedicated male teen readers who know what they want and seem to be eager to continue to read in a series they have started. Just remember that for boys to become fans of fantasy books, they need action in their fantasy, not lengthy character development, or complicated relationships.

Quick 5	Flanagan, John. *The Ranger's Apprentice: The Ruins of Gorlan*. New York: Philomel, 2005. Will is apprenticed to a stern Ranger and must learn the craft of combining stealth and strength in order to battle evil beasts attacking the kingdom. Jacques, Brian. *The Redwall Series.*New York: Philomel, 1986. The adventures and battles of the animal inhabitants of Redwall Abbey—each with its own distinct personality—have thrilled middle school boy readers for years. MacHale, D.J. *The Pendragon Series*. New York: Aladdin, 2002. In the opening title of the series, *The Merchant of Death*, has his Uncle Press tell him he "needs help" and Bobby learns he is a Traveler, one who can ride flumes through time and space. Oppel, Kenneth. *Airborn.* New York: Eos, 2004. Sky pirates, death-defying leaps across space, a 12-year-old hero who cunningly saves the airship while rescuing the girl—what more can a guy reader ask for in fantasy/adventure? Paolini, Christopher. *Eragon. Inheritance, Book One.* New York: Knopf, 2003. Eragon, with the help of his loyal dragon Saphira, realizes he has been chosen to lead the uprising against the rule of the evil King Galbatorix

Fantasy Titles and Series That Have Broad Teen Male Appeal

SCIENCE FICTION—IT'S A BIG UNIVERSE OUT THERE

Science fiction, long a staple of young adult literature, has enjoyed an over 50-year run of connecting with teen readers. The big authors are familiar to librarians—Isaac Asimov, Robert Heinlein, Frank Herbert, L. Ron Hubbard, and Orson Scott Card, to name just a few. This genre was well recognized by adult services before the promotion of young adult services burst on the scene in the 1980s. It appeals to a broad range of readers. But what is science fiction? Is it merely fantasy with some scientific elements involved? Should fantasy and science fiction be grouped into the same genre? Does a teen male reader have to be a techie to appreciate science fiction?

Science fiction has changed greatly since 1952 when Isaac Asimov defined the genre as "that branch of literature which is concerned with the impact of scientific advance upon human beings" (Gilks 2002). Science fiction has evolved from a type of literature concerned with science, to one concerned with the people the science affects. Filled with intriguing "what ifs?" science fiction has a loyal following of readers, perhaps as many in number as those who read fantasy.

A library where I formerly worked as a young adult librarian, had the policy of sticking genre labels on genre books, such as mystery, romance, and so on. For fantasy, the label was a profile of a dragon. For science fiction, the identifying image was a model of an atom with protons and electrons swirling around the nucleus. Of course, both genres have more to offer than just dragons and atom particles, but the symbols convey the difference between the genres. Still, they are difficult to separate in libraries where genres are grouped together for patron convenience. Possibly for shelving convenience, and depending on the size of the collection, many libraries consider the two genres to be too similar to divide.

Science fiction stories usually contain many elements that attract teen males. But for the attraction to happen, there has to be danger involved, often the risk of death in a stark environment far removed from a typical teen's daily life. Teen males are also drawn to science fiction stories where the science—or the humans attempting to control science—has flaws, and the reader knows a disaster will happen. We have seen that many boys prefer to read nonfiction. Because of the scientific aspects, science fiction is a natural crossover from nonfiction. Boys may read a news report about cloning and then be absorbed by Nancy Farmer's book, *The House of the Scorpion* (New York: Antheneum, 2002).

Boys also like to imagine, "what if?" Many science fiction stories take the reader down a path where one small detail has been changed by science; then a chain reaction of disasters rapidly follows. This is the allure of the alternate world type of stories. Harry Turtledove has written a tremendous number of alternate histories. An outstanding example this subgenre is his book, *The Guns of the South: A Novel of the Civil War* (Turtledove, Harry. New York: Ballantine, 1993), a story where the Confederate Army is given AK-47 rifles by time-traveling white supremacists in an attempt to change the racial atmosphere of present time.

The imaginary game of "what if?" can also be played by authors examining what we readers are afraid of today. Is it a widespread plague? Invasion by aliens? Nuclear war? Or will science go mad, marked by human errors, thus regenerating dinosaurs that cannot be controlled? That is the thrilling premise in Michael Crichton's *Jurassic Park* (Crichton, Michael. New York: Ballantine, 1991). Science fiction has many of the same characteristics as thrillers; and can feature man challenging nature or science gone wrong in a suspenseful, face-paced plot. As mentioned previously, the theme of courage and nobility in the face of danger is very attractive to teenage boys entering manhood.

The longevity and continued popularity of science fiction has caused several subgenres to spin-off, creating niches still tied to the overall concepts of science fiction. In their concise article, "Is Science Fiction for You?" that appeared in *Writer* magazine, Marg Gilks, Paula Fleming, and Moria Allen identified over a dozen subgenres of science fiction. All may have some guy-appeal, but whether they appeal to your readers may depend on your particular community and library atmosphere. Let's take a closer look at several of the subgenres that almost consistently appeal to teen males.

Alternative History—Simply addresses the question, "What if an historical event had turned out differently?"

Apocalypitic, Post-Apocalyptic and Holocaust—Focuses on the end of the world, or the world just after "The End."

Cross-genre—defies easy distinctions between science fiction and other genres such as fantasy or horror.

Cyberpunk—set in a high-tech, often bleak, mechanistic and futuristic universe of computers, hackers and computer/human hybrids.

First-contact—explores the initial meeting between humans and aliens.

Hard Science Fiction—is driven more by ideas than characterization. Plausible science and technology are central to the plot.

Humorous Science Fiction—can occur within any of these subgenres or simply spoof a subgenre.

Military Science Fiction—looks at combat in future locations.

Near-Future Science Fiction—science fiction that takes place in the present day or in the next few decades.

Science/Future fantasy—rare now but popular in the 1930s and 1940s, alters, breaks, or ignores known laws or scientific theories for the sake of the story.

Slipstream—deals with mainstream themes but contains a speculative element.

Sociological Science Fiction—is character-driven, with emphasis on social change, personal psychology, and interactions.

Space Operas—often involves good guys "shooting-it-up" with bad guys.

Time travel—characters travel to the past or future, or are visited by travelers from either end of the spectrum.

Science Fiction Subgenres
Source: **Gilks 2002.**

Interestingly, many if not all of these subgenres are also common in graphic novels—an area of young adult reading that is examined later on in this chapter.

Four subgenres that are especially appealing to teen males are:

- Humorous Science Fiction,
- Cyberpunk,
- Military Science Fiction, and
- Time Travel.

Any list of humorous science fiction should include Douglas Adams' *Hitchhiker's Guide to the Galaxy* (Adams, Douglas New York: Harmony Books, 1979), which could easily be considered a top of the list choice for male teens. It is easy for teen boys to get lost in Adams' bizarre world and adventures. However, while a recent movie adaptation of the title may lure readers, the book has been in publication for over two decades. Boy readers, like all teen readers, and most readers in other age groups, prefer more recent titles. With this in mind, consider suggesting *Feed* (Anderson, M. T. Cambridge, MA: Candlewick Press, 2002) by M. T. Anderson, a book that incorporates humor with a coming of age story, along with decisions about rebelling against government control. Scenes like the one where characters party in an antigravity bar on the moon prompt male readers to keep turning pages, even though, as the opening paragraph tells the reader, the moon turned out to suck.

Although *Mortal Engines* (Reeve, Philip. New York: EOS, 2003) is not heavy on computers and technological gadgetry, it does present a bleak view of the future in cyberpunk fashion following a nuclear war. By placing the earth's cities on platforms powered by huge caterpillar treads, author Philip Reeve gives us a story with instant middle-school-boy appeal. The thrilling ending featuring sacrifice and courage is an added bonus. Book Two of the *Hungry City Chronicles*, *Predator's Gold* (Reeve, Philip. New York: EOS, 2004), has the same mechanical allure for boys.

I am personally not a huge fan of lengthy books of any genre, so I cringed when first introduced to Orson Scott Card's *Ender's Shadow* (Card, Orson Scott. New York: TOR, 1999), all 480 pages of it. But at a local university's English Festival, *Ender's Shadow* was on the reading list, and I soldiered on through the text. I was thrilled at my round table discussion where over 30 teens (most of them boys) demanded that I retract any negative thoughts about this book! The teens were passionate in defending Bean's relationship with Ender and how the preparation for battle was so cool. There you have it. Actual testimonies from teens are the best reviews of books and these young men were dedicated to *Ender's Shadow* and were huge fans of anything written by Orson Scott Card.

I am a sucker for time travel stories and I believe many teen males are also. *Timeline* (Crichton, Michael. New York: Alfred A. Knopf, 1999) by Michael Crichton is an excellent example of an adventure story that incorporates time travel. Bandits eager to cut throats, catapults launching pitch over castle walls, broadswords and gruesome dungeons mark this title that will draw teen males. Marketed as an adult novel, this title may not have a home in the young adult section of your library, but it is certainly a book that librarians can suggest to older teen boys.

Quick 5	Farmer, Nancy. *House of the Scorpion*. New York: Atheneum, 2002. By using cloning as a vehicle to promote racism in a future setting dominated by a drug lord, Nancy Farmer has written a novel that involves a life-or-death situation for the main character, a sure bet to attract male readers. Haddix, Margaret Peterson. *Among the Hidden*. New York: Simon & Schuster, 1998. Because he is the illegal third child in a family, Luke has spent 12 years hiding indoors. Upon seeing a face in a neighboring attic window, Luke ventures outside to discover the horrifying truth about the controlling totalitarian government. Sleator, William. *The Last Universe*. New York: Amulet, 2005. Centered on quantum mechanics, but not containing overbearing details about the concept, this title has high boy appeal of entering a dangerous alternate universe, visit other versions by yourself, and return safely. Sleator, William. *Boy Who Couldn't Die*. New York: Amulet, 2004. A book that could be considered more horror than science fiction features Ken, a teen who is afraid of dying and enlists a voodoo woman to remove his soul. Breathless action follows and guys will be thrilled reading about Ken's diving into deep water to first test his immortality and then to recapture his soul. Werlin, Nancy. *Double Helix*. New York: Dial, 2004. Eli's digging into his dying mother's past uncovers genetic-engineering experiments by Dr. Quincy Wyatt and how these experiments are connected to his parents and Eli himself.

More Science Fiction Titles with Guy Appeal

Science fiction continues to thrill many young male readers today. Concepts of genetic engineering, quantum mechanics, or even voodoo seem to have replaced the roots of teen science fiction that featured space travel or visiting other planets. But the constant is still adventure, relying on one's own wits, self-sacrifice, and displaying courage. These traits are what will draw teenage boys to any book; and today's science fiction packs them in.

HORROR, SUSPENSE, MYSTERY—IS IT ALL THE SAME?

Ah, horror novels. These are the books with blood splatters seemingly on every other page, trite Hollywood-type movie scenes of monsters, serial killers, or demons popping out from closets. Often modern young adult horror novels contain cartoon characters with no depth that essentially stay the same throughout the story and allow the action to overwhelm them. Do these books have any value for young adult male readers? Perhaps a better question is: Do young adult males read these books? The answer to the first question is "maybe." The answer to the second question? An emphatic and definite "yes!"

Horror appeals to boys not only because of the "gross-out" factor—the roots of the appeal are deeper. Graham Masterton tells us in his article "Why Horror" that these types of novels dealing with the macabre have other characteristics that attract teen boys. Masterton states, "I think they like horror novels because they depict ordinary people dealing with extraordinary threats. They like to imagine, what would I do if a dark shadow with glowing red eyes appeared in my bedroom at night? What would I do if I heard a sinister scratching inside the walls of my house?" (Masterton 1994).

Another statement about the allure of horror is that it is separated from other genres by the fact that the horror is supernatural, beyond the explainable, the definable, and the containable. It gets its power somewhere else, from a place the author has created for the characters, and for those of us who participate in their adventures (Bodart 1994).

Okay, but what is it about horror novels that teenage boys like? It's simple. These types of books are exciting, action packed rather than character driven, and what description there is within the story usually describes the horror itself, or the suspense leading up to the entrance of the horrific being. In other words, the focus is on the suspense and action rather than the characters. This emphasis on action rather than dialogue and character development draws teen males to horror stories.

On the other hand, not all books with supernatural beings appeal to boys. There are several titles with wide young adult appeal involving ghosts, but these titles are very character-driven and emphasize the losing of a loved one. Two recent titles that come to mind are Alice Sebold's stunning novel, *The Lovely Bones* (Sebold, Alice. Boston: Little, Brown, 2002) and Adele Griffin's *Where I Want to Be* (Griffin, Adele. New York: G. P. Putnam's Sons, 2005).

For boys there has to be an element of danger or a sense that the character feels helpless when first confronted by the horrifying being or situation. Boys like stories in which there is a tiny glimmer of hope, whereby physical strength, courage, or cunning turns the tables on the evil being and escapes the danger. An added bonus is if the male character rescues the girl, who is a love interest for the new hero.

Often, perhaps for convenience, librarians and other book people group horror and suspense together along with mysteries. While some elements may be common to all three groups, they are distinct differences. For example, Agatha Christie's story of 10 people lured to an isolated island and murdered one by one, *And Then There Were None* (Christie, Agatha. New York, Dodd, Mead, 1940) (also titled *Ten Little Indians*), has many mystery and suspense qualities, but cannot be labeled a horror novel due to the lack of a supernatural character. On the other hand, many of Stephen King's books incorporate suspense and mystery and do involve a supernatural event or being. A significant number of King's books continue to draw teen male readers almost 25 years after first published.

| Quick 5 | *Carrie*—Guys' suspicions of the necessity of prom and only bad things can happen there come true as Carrie's fury and revenge descends on the high school event.

The Dead Zone—An ability to see the future and possibly prevent horrible things from occurring appeals to the inner trait of many boys who dream of being heroes.

The Shining—The father flips out and the young boy takes responsibility of saving his mom. Guy appeal theme? You betcha!

'Salem's Lot—Vampires taking over a small town. Sneaking into a "creepy" house. Confronting unspeakable evil. For a teenage boy, what's not to like?

The Long Walk (appearing in The Bachman Books). A test of strength and endurance and weaker participants who lag behind are killed in a walk along U.S. Highway 1. The winner who beats the odds gains unbelievable wealth, which is a sure draw from boys. |

Stephen King's Novels for Boys

In many libraries mysteries are the highest circulating genre for adult readers. But within the genre, there is a lot of diversity. Mysteries can be cozies where the blood and gore are generally not depicted or mentioned, and the person solving the crime is not a law enforcement officer but an amateur (often the most unlikely person to solve the crime). Other mysteries are hard-boiled, where the hero, usually a male, is older, weary of the world, but still clinging to a sense of nobility. Hard-boiled mysteries always involve murder and take place on the mean streets, whether in rural or urban settings. Murders are described in detail and as the killer is hunted down, the suspense mounts.

Quick 5	Child, Lee. *Die Trying.* New York: G. P. Putnam's Sons, 1998.
	Extremely violent, and the body count is very high. Child's hero, Jack Reacher, resembles John Wayne cleaning up the town and older boys will thrill reading about his nobility, courage, and intelligence as he goes about his business.
	Connelly, Michael. *The Poet.* Boston: Little, Brown, 1996. A profiler stalks a serial killer by use of technology. More suspenseful than violent, this book will appeal to male fans of the TV show, CSI.
	Cook, Christopher. *Robbers.* New York: Carroll & Graf, 2000.
	A personal favorite, this gritty crime novel is a fascinating look at hardened criminals on a murderous crime spree and the flawed but noble police officer who pursues them across the dusty Texas landscape.
	Crais, Robert. *L. A. Requiem.* New York: Doubleday, 1999.
	Elvis Cole, a private detective and his loyal friend, Joe Pike, will stop at nothing to track down a serial killer. This title shows how both men's childhoods made them the men they are today, a subplot which will interest teenage boys.
	Hunter, Stephen. *Black Light.* New York: Doubleday, 1996. Bob Lee Swagger dusts off his extraordinary combat skills to discover how his father was murdered in a shootout. Lots of gun action and suspense will draw older teen boys.

Adult Mysteries for Teenage Boys

So mysteries are great reads for guys, especially for adult males. But what about teen mysteries? Do they have guy-appeal? If they do, do they smack of "after-school special," Scooby-Doo, or are a takeoff of The Hardy Boys? Although many libraries and bookstores stock *The Hardy Boys* mysteries, in my experience, either trait is a sure kiss-of-death for sales or circulation. There are not many young adult novels featuring intrepid teen males solving crimes. In the 'tween niche market, Cam Jansen and Encyclopedia Brown may still have a place on the shelves, but for young adults these types of crime-solving books are somewhat rare. The series plot of teens solving crimes as a hobby that might lead to career is fading away from young adult literature. In recent titles with teen boys solving mysteries, the protagonist does not intentionally set out to uncover clues and profile the potential suspects like the junior detective Hardy Boys. The more recent trend is to have a crime committed that somehow affects the teen male character, or involves someone close to them. The main character then becomes pressed to solve the crime/mystery to help a friend or a family member out of trouble.

An excellent example of this type of mystery is *Flush* (Hiaasen, Carl. New York: Alfred A. Knopf, 2005). Teenager Noah Underwood shoulders the responsibility of clearing his father's name, protecting his younger sister, and saving his parents' marriage. He also must prove that a casino boat is illegally dumping waste into Florida bay. Noah solves the crime in spectacular fashion and Hiaasen takes care to make the character an actual teen, not a detective-want-to-be.

	DeFelice, Cynthia. *Death at Devil's Bridge*. New York: Farrar, Straus and Giroux, 2000.
Quick 5	The discovery of a sunken car that flew off of a bridge, a body, and connecting with the village bad boy, places 13-year-old Ben Daggett in the middle of criminal activity. Feinstein, John. *Last Shot: A Final Four Mystery*. New York: Knopf, 2005. Eighth-grade winners of a journalist award, Steve Thomas and Susan Carol Anderson, are given behind-the-scenes access to the NCAA basketball tournament and learn of a game-fixing plot. Realistic sports scenes and the fast-moving pace of the novel will attract middle school guys. Hiaasen, Carl. *Flush*. New York: Knopf, 2005. Noah Underwood hopes to clear his father's name by proving that a casino boat is actually dumping waste into the bay as his father claimed before deliberately sinking the floating gambling hall. Noah is clever, resourceful, and saves the bacon of the clueless adults in the story. Hoobler, Dorothy and Hoobler, Thomas. *In Darkness, Death*. New York: Philomel, 2004. Set in feudal Japan, Judge Ooka and his 14-year-old adopted son, Seikei are asked to investigate the death of Lord Inaba. This title is part of a series where the teen does purposely set out to solve a crime, but the historical setting separates it from other teen detective novels. Plum-Ucci, Carol. *The Body of Christopher Creed*. San Diego, CA: Harcourt, 2000. Torey Adams took his turn picking on and beating up Christopher Creed, but when the boy disappears, Torey becomes obsessed with discovering Christopher's body and the learning ultimate truth of the disappearance.

Mysteries for Teen Guys That Involve Male Teens Solving a Crime

SUSPENSE: A GUY MAGNET

Stories laced with heart-pounding suspense, and that toe-curling tension that keeps readers glued to the book, have great attraction to teen males. Consider what draws guys to suspenseful movies; if that allure is transposed into a print book, then that title will appeal to boys. Cliffhanging chapter endings, a breakneck speed of pacing, and life-threatening danger are some of the traits that make for suspense in any story, whether they are movies or books.

Few young adult titles are actually labeled as "suspense" novels, but many genres today incorporate suspense traits in their storylines. The uncertain outcome, whether the good guys or the bad guys will win, and the narrator or protagonist of the story standing alone and facing danger are story elements common in suspense. Readers fear for the lives of the characters, whether they are in physical danger by being stalked by a serial killer, or actually experiencing psychological problems of their own that very well may lead to suicide.

One of the many attractions to teen readers, and especially male teen readers, of the Harry Potter books is the elements of both physical and psychological suspense that Harry endures. Readers fear for Harry's safety as the ultimate showdown with Lord Voldemort. As the pace of the series accelerates, readers witness Harry in physical danger as well as undergoing psychological stress as he learns more about his relationship with the Dark Lord.

Suspense stories are often set in exotic locations where danger lurks seemingly around every corner. For example, explorers attempting to cross through the Amazon jungle to locate a mythical tree that cures all disease must battle amphibious piranhas, cunning panthers, and enormous crocodiles in James Rollins suspense thriller, *Amazonia* (Rollins, Jame. New York: Avon, 2002). On the other hand, 14-year-old secret agent Alex Rider travels throughout Europe as a spy for British Intelligence as he infiltrates corporate empires attempting to dominate the world by hostile takeovers. The 6 titles in the Alex Rider series by Anthony Horowitz are all great face-paced adventure novels loaded with suspense (*Stormbreaker* (Horowitz, Anthony. New York: Puffin Books, 2001), *Point Blank* (Horowitz, Anthony. New York: Scholastic, 2002), *Skeleton Key* (Horowitz, Anthony. New York: Philomel, 2003), *Eagle Strike* (Horowitz, Anthony. New York: Philomel, 2004), *Scorpia* (Horowitz, Anthony. New York: Philomel, 2005), and *Ark Angel* (Horowitz, Anthony. New York: Philomel, 2006).

For suspense in a teen novel to ring true, the main character must be confronted by a life-threatening situation. This danger can be a blizzard, a serial killer, a ghost, or even a vicious wild animal. This danger places the hero in a situation where the only chance of survival is his own cool head and courage. The theme of a cornered-hero-facing-death can appear in any genre—fantasy, science fiction, historical fiction, or even a problem novel. Suspense is what brings the title to life in the eyes of a teen male and the element of suspense assures the teen reader that this title will be more of an action plot rather than a character-driven novel.

Quick 5	Giles, Gail. *Playing in Traffic*. Brookfield, CT: Roaring Brook, 2004. Danger and suspense can come to a guy by the actions of a weird girl. Skye seduces Matt to do things for her, but the high school senior realizes Skye is dangerous, so dangerous that he might be killed by being with her. Horowitz, Anthony. *Raven's Gate*. New York: Scholastic, 2005. Fourteen-year-old Matt, a troubled teen, finds himself in the care of a coven of witches who are attempting to open a portal to unleash an evil entity. Guys will cheer for Matt, a former loser who becomes the last hope to save the world. McNamee, Graham. *Acceleration*. New York: Wendy Lamb, 2003. The suspense cranks up on each page as 17-year-old Duncan—haunted by a past failure to save a female swimmer—feels he alone must stop a serial killer who is stalking a woman in the subway of Toronto. Mikaelsen, Ben. *Touching Spirit Bear*. New York: HarperCollins, 2001. Angry, defiant and smug, Cole Matthews finds himself in a life-or-death situation on an isolated island after being mauled by a bear. Myers, Walter Dean. *Monster*. New York: HarperCollins, 1999. The legal fate—death penalty or life in prison—of Steven Harmon is in limbo until the very end of this ground breaking novel about a teen on trial for murder.

Teen Novels with Suspense That Appeal to Teen Males

GRAPHIC NOVELS—THE COMIC BOOK GROWS UP

A standard greeting between friends who are readers may soon be adjusted by bibliophiles everywhere. The phrase, "Read any good books lately?" in the next few years may switch to, "Looked at any good books lately?" The universal appeal and continuing explosion of influence of graphic novels very well may change the world of reading, especially for teens and particularly for teen boys.

Beginning in the early years of the twentieth-century and on into the 1930s when superhero comics hit the market, teen boys were drawn to the colorful artwork and thrilling tales found in the pages of comic books, much to the chagrin of teachers. Today's graphic novels are different, but how different? Should librarians and professionals working closely with teens continue to view graphic novels as literature's twisted cousin?

Before evaluating the place of graphic novels in today's teen collections, let's review some definitions. The terms can be confusing to anyone just beginning to explore what graphic novels are all about. To clear up confusion, I offer these three basic definitions, gleaned from attending workshops over the years. Hopefully, this will help you start to build a working knowledge of graphic novels.

> *Comic Books*—a single-issue comic offering an installment for an established series; it can be very glossy and usually is an episode of approximately 20 pages.
>
> *Trade Paperbacks*—In a single volume, several issues of a comic book series are gathered and produced to help establish continuity from one episode to the next.
>
> *Graphic Novel*—A story, either part of a series or standing by itself, told with a combination of words and sequential drawings or illustrations appearing either in black, and white, or full color.

For the purposes of this section, I will refer to all the books as "graphic novels," which streamlines the definition to mean books dominated with illustrations.

A more formal description of a graphic novel is offered in Julia Campbell's article, "Picture This: Inside the Graphic Novel." Contributor Francisca Goldsmith, a librarian at Berkeley (California) Public Library offers this description, "Graphic novels use images and words to tell a story that has a beginning, a middle, and an end. It is different from a comic book in that the story ends. The flow of the words and the images work together—you can't just look at the pictures and not read the words" (Campbell 2004).

In spite of its current popularity, the uncertainty of the place of graphic novels in the literary universe continues. I have been told (by qualified book professionals) that graphic novels are all pornographic, have limited literary value, are trash, not worthy of full cataloging, are ephemeral material, and have no place in a teen area so close to the children's collection.

The prejudice against graphic novels and the ongoing debate of their purpose could produce dozens of articles and books. This debate, better suited for another professional title, shall be put aside to concentrate on the connection between graphic novels and teenage male readers. Instead, let's focus on fitting graphic novels into your teen collection and discussing how you can use titles in this format to motivate boys to read.

The fact is, graphic novels are every bit of a preferred format of reading by a group of library patrons as board and pop-up books are for preschool children, or large print and audio books are for elderly patrons.

Misconceptions about graphic novels continue in libraries and schools where professionals consider them only to be useful for readers who struggle with vocabulary. Other book people only see the value of graphic novels for undereducated readers who have trouble figuring out intricate storylines.

Adding to her statements contained in Julia Campbell's "Picture This: Inside the Graphic Novel" article, Francesca Goldsmith offers another point of view. She tells us, "There is a lack of information and naiveté in people who believe that graphic novels are for readers with short attention spans. You have to have a pretty solid attention span to weave back and forth between the images and the text."

The same article incorporates a quote from Steve Weiner, author of *Faster Than a Speeding Bullet: The Rise of the Graphic Novel*, who informs us, "You have to think about it as just another form of writing instead of just a comic book. You'll get serious books, silly books, and everything in-between. Just think of it as a new way to tell stories" (Campbell 2004).

With sales figures in the hundreds of millions of dollars, in the United States alone, annual sales of manga now approach $140 million, graphic novels are being read, purchased, and embraced by readers. As Michael Cart states, "Love it or hate it, the form is clearly no longer a novelty" (Cart 2005).

Yet educators still hesitate to embrace graphic novels. An underlying bias lingers on, a bias that perpetuates the opinion that reading graphic novels is just better than reading nothing at all. In a *Reading Today* article about using graphic novels in the classroom, Jacquie McTaggart states, "Clearly comics and graphic novels do not constitute what most of us consider to be good literature. However before we can make kids read what we want them to, we must first make them want to read. If hooking kids on books requires us to do it their way, via comics and graphic novels, so be it. The end justifies the means" (McTaggert 2005).

In the meantime, you know that meeting teens on their home turf works. Teens, especially boys, become excited about reading when given some freedom of choice. A 16-year-old guy informed me recently as I asked him about what is so appealing about a nonfiction book about jewelry in the hip-hop world, "This is what we are all about—this is what our age group sees everyday." The same thinking should be applied in providing graphic novels for teens in any reading atmosphere.

I'm not suggesting you crate up books by classic authors such as Steinbeck, Faulkner, and Cather; but I am suggesting you incorporate and acknowledge a new wave of reading style. It may be just the thing to create a spark for male readers. As Jacquie McTaggert continues, "Teachers using these tools say many of their reluctant readers, especially boys, are being transformed from 'I hate to read' kids into 'This book rocks' students" (McTaggert 2005).

Manga—Reading Material from the Pacific Rim

If anyone still thinks that teens don't read, and that there is little interest in reading, and that this generation is only about the Internet and video games, here are some facts about manga. In 2004, it was estimated that publishers released about 1,000 manga titles and the sales topped $170 million (Manga Bonanza 2004).

Manga, graphic novels in the Japanese style of artwork, have been distributed in the United States for some time, but it has only been in the past 5 years or so that the explosion has really hit the American market. (Remember, manga are the print graphic novels that use the Japanese style of artwork; anime are the video versions that are shown electronically. Several series appear in both manga and anime formats.)

Manga offers something for almost all teen readers from adventure and romance to fantasy and even sports. Guys flock to their favorite series. If you have the opportunity to witness guys with manga, take it. You might learn more about what appeals to them—and it may surprise you. The guys I talk to in my anime club are much more interested in the storylines rather than the artwork. I was anticipating the exact opposite.

What about manga series appeals to guys? First and foremost, swordplay. They love the action and violence. Two young men, Mario and William, picked *Chronicles of the Cursed Sword* as their favorite manga series because "There's lots of action and violence with swords, demons and stuff." Other manga hooks for boys are *Ninjas* and the wide use of martial arts. These things are the key to their worship of the two series, *Flame of Recca* and *Naruto*.

Interestingly, these guys also like the comedy that manga offers. During showings at our anime club meetings, I often find myself clueless at why the teens are laughing uncontrollably. Two series they mentioned as being great examples of manga style comedy are *Inu Yasha* (Kagome can put a spell on Inu Yasha and there's no way he can dodge it, and *Ranma 1/2* which in their words, "Has great comedy and romance").

It is true that manga always has illustrations that are essential to the story. However, the only teens who discuss the artwork with me are older guys who are totally into the manga books. They can tell you in detail, why certain drawings are more attractive than others. But based on my informal interviews with teen males, I am fairly positive that the allure of manga titles for guys are the storylines, especially those that involve a high level of action.

Quick 5	Arakawa, Hiromu. *Fullmetal Alchemist.* The epic journey of Al and Ed, two brothers trying to put their bodies and their lives back together, includes loyalty, humor, and great battle scenes. Hirano, Kohta. *Hellsing.* Vampire hunter Alucard, wears an oversized hat and a duster that swirls dashingly as he blows bad guys to smithereens with his arsenal of enormous firearms. Kishimoto, Masashi. *Naruto.* Manga doesn't have to be total violence to attract male readers. Naruto is all about the fun side of manga and middle school boys love it. Sanjo, Riku. *Beet the Vandel Buster.* Guys cheer for the heroic Beet, a young boy setting off on a quest to defeat the Vandels who are monsters terrorizing the world. Watsuki, Nobuhiro. *Rurouni Kenshin.* This longrunning manga series features many things that attract guys, humor, drama, fighting, and even romance.

Manga Series with Guy Appeal

Graphic Novels from the United States—Not the Same Old, Same Old

Although both manga and Western style of graphic novels have been on the market for over 40 years, most librarians and adults are more familiar—and more comfortable—with the Western type of comics. Sometimes referred to as "traditional" comics, these are the titles that predominately feature superheroes. Not only are the superheroes shown with rippling muscles and performing astounding feats, they also often single-handedly take on an evil villain who is bent on destroying a city, or possibly even a region of the world. Powerful characters slug it out, often suspended in midair (many superheroes can defy gravity). The battles are illustrated with violent, haymaker-type of punches that knock the characters across streets and throw brick walls. Large bold-stroked letters add sound effects that readers can voice out loud (Zonk! Pow! and Smash!).

Here lies the essential allure of Western graphic novels for boys: they have many fight scenes. However, on closer examination, Western graphic novels contain many other story elements that have high guy appeal as well. The superhero often has a deep sense of loyalty to a city, or a group of people. He often willingly risks his life to protect these people or fight for an abstract value. A good superhero does not ask questions, he does things. This is what boys long to do. During their teenage years, boys want to be someone, someone who stands out from the crowd, but is not a jerk and is admired by all. The genius of many Western graphic novel creators is that they disguise the superhero as an everyday type of guy, which makes the heroic deeds, when they occur, even more astounding to the teen male reader.

The generations of readers of Western graphic novels seem to be clicking over. Today's teens are aware of the old guard—Superman, Batman, and the Hulk—but they like to mix in, and even seem more enthusiastic about the X-Men, the Invincibles, The Goon, and Spawn. Keep in mind that the popularity of superhero graphic novel series often coincides with movies that are released. For example, the Fantastic Four experienced a tremendous boost in popularity when the film version was released; as did Spiderman and Hellboy when movies based on those characters came out. Beyond the worshiped hero, other guy reader attractions are there. In these comics, violence, strength, courage, and the ability to place others before self will continue to lure teen males to the pages of graphic novels.

<table>
<tr>
<td rowspan="5">Quick
5</td>
<td>

McFarlane, Todd. *Spawn.*
>From the depths of Hell, Spawn searched New York City for clues to his horrific existence. Guys love the nobility of this tortured hero.

Mignola, Mike. *Hellboy.*
>Hellboy has a right fist of granite, carries a huge pistol and is the world's greatest paranormal investigator. This graphic novel character brings loads of guy appeal.

Niles, Steve. *30 Days of Night.*
>A bloodthirsty gang of vampires attack Barrow, Alaska, bent on spending a month of carnage before the sun appears again.

Powell, Eric. *The Goon.*
>The Goon, an old-style enforcer, just has to stomp zombies now and then but his other foes include regular guys.

Vaughn, Brian K. *Y: The Last Man.*
>A disease wipes out all the males in the world except Yorick Brown. Oh, the fantasies guys envision while reading this graphic novel. But beware, not all the women desire Yorick!

</td>
</tr>
</table>

Western Graphic Novel Series That Appeal to Teen Males with Characters Other Than Traditional Superheroes

HISTORICAL FICTION—DO GUYS APPRECIATE THE PAST?

Young adult librarians have the task of suggesting and even "pushing" books to teens. In my experience, one of the tougher genre sells for teen males is historical fiction. I have found that many teen boys would just rather read a nonfiction book about the person or event than tackle a made-up story constructed around the historical situation. But since boys like to do things that involve physical activity, create things, or take things apart, there's still hope with historical fiction. If unable to physically accomplish these tasks, boys like to read about these activities. They can analyze and place themselves in the role of the character. Many boys dream and imagine what they would have done differently than the main character. Often this "role-play through reading" involves a test of courage or a passage into manhood.

In recent years, teachers have begun to spice up their history lessons by incorporating historical fiction titles into the required reading. Why? Why take a potentially exciting topic, dissect it, and overanalyze it, and then subject a reader to a test on the book's concepts. I cannot think of a more straight-to-the-heart method of destroying any joy of reading for a male teen. A more guy-friendly approach would be to offer a list of suggested historical fiction titles on a suggested topic, rather than to place a grade on a required reading of a particular historical fiction novel. This is a situation where cooperation between the school librarian, the public librarian, and the teacher is essential to form a suggested booklist that will interest males and females.

To explain what I am speaking about when mentioning historical fiction, I offer these loose definitions. Historical fiction can be written in any of these general methods.

- The author writes about an actual person from history and surrounds him or her with fictional events or circumstances that do not have to be verified by research.

- The author writes about an actual event that occurred in history and places fictional characters in that setting where they become part of the history-making event.

- The author writes about an era, or a span of time, and constructs a setting with historical elements that were common to that era but are not pinpointed to an exact month or year. Often these settings have both fictional and real characters weaving in and out of the story. Other times the actual person from history will have somewhat of a cameo appearance.

Types of Historical Fiction

Books featuring any of these approaches can be classified as historical fiction. The draw to teen males largely depends on the historical character or event. In my experience, teen males would much rather read about a famous male from history rather than about a female.

What types of historical fiction has guy appeal? I've observed many boys showing a huge interest in war stories and the rites of passage males have traditionally undertaken in battle. With the sixtieth anniversary of the ending of World War II in the recent news, many boys are curious to read about guys in the past who were shipped off to horrifying conditions when they were in their teens. I have presented historical fiction novels set during World War II or a specific battle in that world war and many times gained feedback from guys who tell me, "I saw that on the History Channel!"

For many decades teen males have enjoyed adventure stories. The enduring allure of Robert Louis Stevenson's *Treasure Island* is the danger Jim Hawkins faces as a teen on an adventure far away from his home. *Treasure Island* is a historical story, in which boys can put themselves in place of the character and wonder what they would do to survive. An historical fiction story works best for male readers when the teen character is placed in a dangerous situation, where the male protagonist (boys prefer to read about males) must survive the circumstances brought on by others or by a natural catastrophe. And he must either use his physical strength or his quick mind to triumph over the danger. The combination of a recognizable historical event—or era—plus a high degree of danger and adventure is an outstanding draw for teen male readers.

Quick 5	Bruchac, Joseph. *Code Talker.* New York: Dial, 2005. As a former Navajo Code Talker, Ned Begay tells his grandchildren how he hung on to his Navajo consciousness and traditions even in dealing with fear, loneliness, and the horrors of Guadalcanal, Bougainville, Guam, Iwo Jima, and Okinawa.
	Hughes, Dean. *Soldier Boys.* New York: Atheneum, 2001. Teen warriors, Spencer from the United States and Dieter from Germany, are on a collision course to meet in the frozen ground of the Battle of the Bulge.
	Lawrence, Iain. *B for Buster.* New York: Delacorte, 2004. Kak enlists in the Royal Air Force to escape his abusive and alcoholic father. What he did not count on was the terrifying bombing runs over Germany where death is simply a matter of bad luck.
	Salisbury, Graham. *Eyes of the Emperor.* New York: Wendy Lamb, 2005. Eddy Okubo is a Japanese-American teen serving in the military when the bombing of Pearl Harbor occurs. Eddy's job? He is to become "bait" for attack dogs because the government's thinking is that Japanese smell different from Americans.
	Wilson, Diane Lee. *Black Storm Comin'.* New York: Margaret K. McElderry, 2005. Only 12-years-old, Colton Wescott becomes the man of his family as they journey west. To survive hunger, and the racism directed at his mixed-race family, Colton gets a job as a Pony Express Rider. His route is the most dangerous leg of the entire trail.

Historical Fiction Novels That Thrill Teen Males

SPORTS STORIES—NOT JUST THE ESPN HIGHLIGHTS

With the wide participation of boys playing Little League baseball, Pee Wee football, and organized games of basketball, it makes sense that boys are interested in sports stories. As boys grow older they may abandon their participation in sports, but with television broadcasting a huge variety of sports 24/7, again potential interest in sports stories is there. The Super Bowl, March Madness, the World Series, and the words playoffs all stir boys' competitive souls. Throw in video games that are action-packed such as Madden football and it is easy to see that teens, especially boys, are bombarded by sports. Of course, oversized and highly visual nonfiction books about sports are a big draw for teenage boys. Do novels about sports have the same attraction? Yes and no.

Sports books have been staples of young adult fiction for years. The stories of John R. Tunis, William Campbell Gault, and Claire Bee have been read by boys since the 1930s. These sports books introduced problems teens had with sports; conflicts with teammates, internal conflicts about not being good enough to make the team, and boys coming from "the wrong side of the tracks" to compete against privileged opponents. The majority of the pages featured action on the field or court and very little about what was happening to the characters off the field of play.

The popularity and publication of sports stories faded sometime during the 1970s and 1980s, perhaps because publishers were producing so many nonfiction sports titles with glossy photographs. Magazines such as *Sports Illustrated* increased their promotions by targeting the teen audience and began to become the reading material of choice by teens wishing to read about sports. For a time it was difficult to recommend a quality sports novel to teens.

Although there were many attempts at writing sports stories, sometimes the authors just did not write realistic sports scenes and the books were not popular. That is changing. While the authors of the 1940s wrote of honor and fair play while competing, today's sports books don't show a tremendous amount of action on the court or field. Some of the best sports books produced in recent years in fact only contain a few pages of sports action. These sports books can arguably be classified as problem novels as the male teen character experiences a wide range of problems from crime, drug and alcohol abuse, to rocky relationships with girls.

Several recent sports novels feature outstanding writing. The stories are exciting, the action scenes are very realistic, and the slang that happens during the games is spot on. Currently there seems to be more young adult novels about baseball or basketball than football. Perhaps the action of a violent football game is difficult for authors to translate to paper. Recent movies about high school sports only help stir the interest. Several sports movies were books first. *Friday Night Lights: A Town, a Team, and a Dream* (Bissinger, H.G. Reading, MA: Addison-Wesley Pub. Co., 1990) is an example of a great nonfiction book that was made into a popular movie. Steer boys who are interested in sports to these fresh and great titles.

Quick 5	Coy, John. *Crackback.* New York: Scholastic, 2005. One of the few football stories that puts the reader right on the field and part of the action. The players' decisions about steroid use is absolutely right on time.
	de la Pena, Matt. *Ball Don't Lie.* New York: Delacorte, 2005. Mentioned earlier as a problem novel that has high guy-appeal, this book about the rough life of a streetballer possibly contains some of the more realistic pick-up basketball scenes in any young adult novel.
	Hughes, Pat. *Open Ice.* New York: Wendy Lamb, 2005. High school hockey star Nick Taglio suffers a concussion that ends his career on the ice, and then he discovers the betrayal of his girlfriend and friends.
	Volponi, Paul. Bla*ck and White* New York: Viking, 2005. Social issues of inner city teens attempting armed robbery mix in with great basketball scenes in this riveting tale of challenged friendship.
	Waltman, Kevin. *Learning the Game.* New York: Scholastic, 2005. Nate hopes to become a starter on his school's basketball team but his dream is derailed when he and his teammates take part in robbing a fraternity house.

Outstanding Sports Fiction for Guys

Adult professionals working closely with teens often argue that more girls than boys can be called readers of fiction. The reasons for this are many; and there is no simple solution of turning teen males into avid fiction readers. However, you can start by recognizing that the world of fiction contains many distinct genres, many of which have some appeal to teen boys. Attracting males to fiction can be accomplished by linking fiction books with nonfiction titles on the same subject. Displays about sports can combine fiction, nonfiction, and magazine titles. Audio books may also be incorporated when forming displays of a particular genre.

Ultimately, one of the most effective methods of directing teen guys to fiction is to meet them on their own turf. Form a connection with your nearby school media specialists and make arrangements to present to English classes some of the more alluring books recently published. Of course, it is up to you to read and familiarize yourself with the latest and best books, both fiction and nonfiction. We'll discuss how to conduct school visits and how to engage teen males during booktalks in Chapter 7.

REFERENCES

Bodart, Joni Richards. "In Defense of Horror Fiction." *Book Report* (March/April 1994): 12.

Campbell, Julia. "Picture This: Inside the Graphic Novel." *Literary Cavalcade* (May 2004): 18–20).

Cart, Michael. "A Graphic Novel Explosion." *Booklist* (March 15, 2005): 1301.

Gilks, Marg, Fleming, Paula, and Allen, Moira. "Is Science Fiction for You?" *Writer* (November 2002): 36.

Herald, Diana Tixier. *Teen Genreflecting: A Guide to Reading Interests* (Westport, CT: Libraries Unlimited, 2003).

McTaggert, Jacquie. "Using Comics and Graphic Novels to Encourage Reluctant Readers." *Reading Today* (October/November 2005): 46.

"Manga Bonanza." *Publisher's Weekly* (December 6, 2004): 38.

Masterton, Graham. "Why Horror?" *Writer* (July 1994): 107.

Miller, Laura. "A Good Book Should Make You Cry." *New York Times* (August 22, 2004).

"Nonfiction Honor List." *VOYA* (August 2005): 185–187.

The Plain Dealer. Section A2 (May 30, 2005). "One of the Last Living WWI Vets Rides in Style Today."

Webster's Third New International Dictionary of the English Language, Unabridged (Springfield, MA: Merriam-Webster, 1986).

The Week 5(220) (August 12, 2005): 18.

Young Adult Library Services Association-Booklists & Book Awards. http://www.ala.org/yalsa/booklistsawards/booklistsbook.htm.

Chapter 6

ENGAGING TEEN MALES IN LIBRARY PROGRAMMING AND TEEN ADVISORY BOARDS

Recently a query was posted on the Ohio young adult listserv questioning librarians about their attitudes about library programs for young adults. It came as no surprise. The answers were varied and covered a full range of attitudes. Several librarians stated that they enjoy constructing and presenting programs and feel they really connected to their teen populations through programming. Other librarians conveyed disillusionment about the importance and benefit of teen programs. A follow-up posting on the listserv queried librarians about their worst programming disasters. This question produced a flurry of responses detailing horrifying situations. Noticeably absent in this informal online discussion was any feedback about teen programming that appeared to be simply neutral. There seemingly is no gray area concerning librarians' attitudes about the emphasis of programming.

Like it or not, teen programming is here to stay and has become a cornerstone task for young adult librarians. There may be a heavy or light emphasis on programming in any given library, but rare is the library that does nothing in the way of offering programs for teens. The degree of emphasis stems partly from a library's administration, but the true emphasis comes from the young adult librarian's own creativity and energy levels. Another important factor can be a sparse programming or supply budget.

Before we explore some of the specific ways to engage teen males with programs and outreach services, let's examine the pros and cons of out-reach programming. Our focus here is on programs offered inside the library facility, not traveling out of the building. (Traveling to do outreach services is covered in Chapter 8.)

WHAT'S WRONG WITH TEEN PROGRAMMING?

When first hired as a young adult librarian, you may find yourself work-ing under an administration that wants to see the library sponsor as many programs as possible. Many teen librarians eventually leave teen services to enter another area of library work simply because of unreasonable ex-pectations about producing teen programs. On the other hand, teens just may need a program that will bring them to the library. Teen programming can be a very interesting double-bladed sword.

Perceived Competition with the Children's Department

Teen librarians sometimes feel pressured to offer as many programs for teens as the children's department provides for preschool through sixth-grade children.

In the library context, comparing the two age categories is a mistake, partly due to the fact that the needs for the two groups are vastly different. Avoid the trap of competing with the children's department on the number and success of programs. Of course, many library administrators only look at the numbers; that is, how many programs were offered and what were the attendance figures of those programs. If that is the only formal means of evaluation for your library programs, then teen services will always finish behind the children's department.

In my experience, the children's department usually is staffed with more employees and has more money budgeted for programming. Due to the ages of the children, the programs are shorter in length, sometimes 20–30 minutes whereas a teen program may continue for 2 hours. In addition, parents generally bring their children to the library. Teens most often find their own way, or are dropped off by the adults. The logistics of simply getting to the library accounts for a huge difference between the age groups, with teens at a big disadvantage.

The Teen Services Position is Often a Split Job

As noted earlier, teen librarians often find themselves tacked on to another department, either adult or children's services. And, in a time of tight budgets, they may find that the teen position is a part-time job, perhaps only offering 20 hours a week. Designing a program takes time that the teen librarian may not have, due to the nature of their job. In addition to less time, there may be less money in the teen program budget (if there is one at all) and the lack of funding can limit how much programming you can accomplish.

The Library May Not Receive a Group of Teens with Open Arms

In some libraries, the sad reality is that the teens are simply unwelcome, especially when in large groups. Even the best efforts of the administration and teen librarian in promoting services to young adults can be undone by an insensitive circulation employee or security person. You may find yourself having to send specific notifications to other areas of the library that on a certain date and time, a teen program will take place. This of course can be labeled professional courtesy, but too often this notification, if verbalized, is often received with a groan. As we know, teens pick up on negative attitudes. And if the group of teens is mostly guys, (who tend to be bigger and louder)—the greater the chance that the staff will react less positively.

WHAT'S RIGHT WITH TEEN PROGRAMMING?

The public library is a community service facility. Teen patrons deserve the opportunity to experience things they may not have access to in their homes. A well-designed teen program can bring both girls and boys into the library and make them aware of what their library and community can offer.

The Forty Developmental Assets Tell Us This is a Good Thing

Where does your duty as a librarian end? Should we as professionals dip into tasks that are almost a copy of work a social worker accomplishes? I have found myself both in the middle and on the fringes of this debate with my co-workers in my library system, and while attending workshops with other teen librarians. Okay, the behind-the-desk routine is just about over, but what outreach work is off-limits for the teen librarian? Is there a difference between counseling and listening? When do you give teen advice about a revealed problem? Should you help a teen land a job? These are very difficult decisions and questions. Perhaps it comes down to the role of the library in the community.

The Search Institute has produced a list of 40 Developmental Assets essential to raising successful young people. A complete listing of these assets can be found at http://www.search-institute.org/assets. Many of the assets directly address a lifelong commitment to learning and a sense of identity that helps to empower the young person. The Search Institute also states that young people need to experience support and care from both their families and other agencies in the community. These are certainly valued goals that every professional working with teens should strive to accomplish.

A solid and well-planned library program that dovetails with the 40 Developmental Assets can greatly reward you and the teens with a positive experience. However, I encourage you to consider enlisting outside agencies that are experts in a particular area to run teen programs. For example, it would be a mistake, as a librarian, to conduct an "Identify the Warning Signs of Abuse" workshop/program. Even with the best intentions, statements made in this hypothetical program may be taken as advice that should not be given by a librarian. Many agencies in a wide variety of communities that deal with teens are quite gracious about presenting for free. Use their expertise: it is valuable.

When planning a program, ask yourself, will this program benefit teens? Is there someone in the community able to do this program better than I can? And, perhaps most importantly, am I stepping too far outside the box and inviting backlash about intruding into a teen issue I am not qualified to address?

Problems can also arise from the administration that wishes to "connect" with the community. While a goal of having the library being front and center to the population, an administrator's overzealousness may place you as a teen librarian in a situation that you are totally unprepared to accomplish. Evaluate the entire situation before plunging ahead.

That said, a quality teen program that incorporates community volunteers and dispenses information in an atmosphere that is separate from, and not as rigid as, school may be a great boost to any teens' library experience.

The Library's Image May Be Enhanced by Teen Programs

The days when librarians sat behind a large desk waiting to dispense knowledge if asked are certainly waning, if not over. With the continued proliferation of home computer use and people staying home to utilize their entertainment systems, the library's role in the community is undergoing sweeping changes. The teens are out there in similar numbers as they have always been, but there are more distractions that keep them out of the library. Programming is one way to get them back into the building; and once in the library, they may say, "Hey, this was pretty cool, are you going to do it again?" Administrators love to remind us that teens are the future taxpayers and serving this patron base with a positive experience may in the future lead to a yes vote on a levy ballot.

Teen Programming Puts the Professional in Touch with the Teen Patron

Working at a help or readers' advisory desk allows you to become aware of the reading tastes of different patrons. The hottest titles are placed on reserve and your collection development department can use this information to construct a collection that results in high circulation figures. The same thinking may be applied to programming. Teens are the patron group that is in tune with what is popular now, 10 minutes ago, and what is "out" as of yesterday. To be part of a program (ideally suggested by teens or a teen advisory board) allows you to know what interests the teens and how the libraries collection can be developed around those interests. In addition, teens may suggest programs that are particularly attractive to guys.

RoseMary Honnold, an outstanding young adult librarian, of Coshocton Public Library of Ohio, has written two especially helpful professional books on teen programming: *101 + Teen Programs That Work* and *More Teen Programs That Work*. She also has a Web page, See YA AROUND, which can be located at http://www.cplrmh.com. When justifying teen programs, she says, "Programs also give librarians an opportunity to interact with, educate, and entertain teens, while providing positive role models and experiences" (Honnold 2003).

Another title, which is included in the Libraries Unlimited series "Professional Guides for Young Adult Librarians" and written by Valerie A. Ott, is *Teen Programs with Punch: A Month-by-Month Guide*. This book provides many suggestions of how young adult librarians can form connections with teen patrons through programming.

Earlier I mentioned that many young adult librarians become disillusioned with programming. This problem may stem from the one-person show phenomenon, which is often the case in teen librarianship.

As a teen librarians, you may find yourself overwhelmed with developing the initial idea or brainstorm for the program, implementing the program's plan, and being expected to facilitate the setup for the program, including paperwork, room reservation, and so on. Depending on the size of your library, even the publicity for the program may be up to you; if you're in a larger library system, you may have to sell the publicity vision to a graphics department or a public relations department.

Once all the preliminary setup work is done and the big day has arrived, you "cross your fingers," hoping that teens will show up. The program is presented and then the cleanup begins. To do all these tasks for every program can easily lead to burn out. A children's department staff can share these tasks, but teen departments are often staffed only by one person. If that's the case in your library, programs can be a tremendous amount of work; efforts and the "rewards" might be questioned.

With the overall increase of services to teens, burn out is not a recent phenomenon. In 1997, Mary K. Chelton warned of teen librarian burn out in her book, *Excellence in Library Services to Young Adults*. The author states, "It is not uncommon for YA staff to burn out from the energy drain of fighting to attract the kids on one hand, and keep the bureaucracy off their backs on the other" (Chelton 1997).

To avoid the potential drawbacks of teen programming, good planning is essential. It is wise to "pick the battles you can win." Organize yourself, decide what you can do, what budget can be contributed to the program, and try to gather teens' opinions before deciding on what programs to present.

DECIDING THE MAIN FOCUS OF A PROGRAM

When planning a program, your first task is to understand the traits of your audience. Teens are not the same in every area of the country. If your goal is to attract guys to the program, then determine what is of interest to the guys in your service area. To simply plug in a program idea that has been described as a success during a professional workshop may be a failure back at your library. This is a good reason to listen to the local teens (hopefully including teen males) either by informal chats near the teen area or surveying a teen advisory board (or the teen population) for ideas.

The Librarian as an Entertainer

Before getting to the nuts and bolts of program planning, decide what or who will be the main focus of the program. I find myself in awe of children's librarians who are the main focus of their programs. To hold the children's interest during story times, they sing songs, clap and keep a beat, play simple instruments, and change their voices like actors in a play.

A teen audience is different. Today, librarians find themselves competing with online gaming, cable TV, music videos, and iPods to capture the interest of the teens. I suppose there are teen librarians who are talented enough to sing, play an instrument, and perform for the teens thus becoming an "entertainer" and the focus of the program, but a teen audience is a little harder to please than a group of 3-year-olds. In addition, this would likely create a situation where the program is considered a version of a children's program attended by older patrons.

You could argue that the "fun" of a teen karaoke night is to sing poorly, including a performance by the teen librarian. However, earlier in this book, I mentioned that guys avoid anything that makes then appear weak. To be potentially embarrassed in front of other teens he doesn't even know may be a disaster, real or perceived, to a young man. I believe performance-type programs, such as karaoke night, usually work better if the teens are familiar with each other. Library systems that draw from different areas where the teens meet each other for the first time at the library program may need "icebreakers" so the teens can get a handle on the different personalities in the room. Teens, especially guys, do not want to come to a library program and end up being humiliated.

The Program Drives the Program

Since I am not one of the fine arts talented librarians, I need to figure out a focus other than myself for a program. That focus is usually a "what" rather than the "who" of the program's emphasis.

Where the program itself drives the event, there is more potential for guy participation and the potential embarrassment factor is removed. When the program has a craft-type emphasis, it often becomes successful. That's the good news. The bad news is that it may take some selling to get a guy to attend a craft program. It is not unheard of however. It mostly depends on the craft being made. If it is totally "girly" (such as beading or braiding), well, the guys will just hang out somewhere else. Interestingly, craft programs attended by guys in my system are ones where cards, either for Mother's Day or Valentine's Day, are constructed.

Programs that have guy appeal focus on role-playing games, such as "Magic, the Gathering," or "Dungeons & Dragons." The popularity of these games fluctuates from community to community, so consult the teens that visit your library before launching a game-based program.

Board games such as Monopoly and Risk seemingly attract more boys than girls, especially if the competition of a tournament is involved. Chess can be very intriguing for boys, and many schools have formed chess clubs. If you're planning a tournament of any kind, be sure to separate the teens by age or have a registration where they state their level of expertise. A tournament is no fun if a senior high school expert player beats a first-time seventh-grade player in three moves.

In our library an all-male draw, suggested by the young men, was a video game challenge on Fridays. The guys brought in their own equipment (PlayStation2) and the library simply provided the TV monitors.

A gaming tournament by a LAN (Local Access Network) can be planned if enough equipment is available. This requires a lab-type situation with at least six to eight computer terminals or laptops. Librarians who sponsor these game nights like to utilize a meeting room, so the guys can spread out and move around. The program just does not work if equipment is unavailable. Again, this takes cooperation from the rest of the library staff, as well as planning and setup.

Many teen guys come to the library simply to get their Japanese comic fix. They love to read manga and stories about sword fights and ninjas. They log on to the library's computers to hit the best anime sites. The natural progression of this trend is to form an organized Anime Club or meeting. Teens love to discuss the artwork of a series, the conflict the character is experiencing, and to voice their predictions of what will happen in the next episode. If these things happened in a book discussion of a popular hardback novel, then that group would be deemed a huge success. Many anime companies wish to promote their products, and provide preview DVDs simply by having anime clubs registering and filling out questionnaires and surveys.

Bringing in Outsiders

Earlier in this chapter, I suggested the practical benefits of enlisting a community expert to conduct a program on a specific topic. Without question, from publicity to the actual event, the presenter should be the focus of the program. In this case the teen librarian assumes the role of an organizer and planner. Set up every detail beforehand, so the outside person can do his or her program and leave with a positive experience. Types of outside performers who come to present at the library are: authors, college representatives, representatives from local service organizations such as the YMCA or Red Cross, or local businesspeople such as those who work at car dealerships, comic book shops or hobby shops that deal with sophisticated toys. Utilizing your community resources is a recommended method by the 40 Developmental Assets, to make teens aware of what the community offers and how they can benefit from the experience.

The bad news is that although many of these outside presenters volunteer their time, others may charge an hourly fee, or at least want to be paid for their transportation. You may have to debate whether the sometimes tough-to-measure benefits justify the cost. Your first instinct might be to have a registration process to determine how many teens will be attending. Asking for preregistration may or may not be helpful. Teens may sign up weeks in advance, but not show up on the day; or they may not sign up and arrive in droves. In our system, we never turn any teen away from a program (unless he or she is disruptive).

Author visits are a huge draw for teens, but their fees can sometimes be prohibitive. This is especially true for authors who have written award-winning books or those whose books have been adapted into movies. A modest honorarium for a teen author visit seems to be around $750 a day; and the high end is about $5,000 a day. On the other hand, many libraries have budgeted money for such visits during October's Teen Read Week.

THE BIG-TICKET ITEMS—SYSTEM-WIDE PROGRAMS

Depending on the size of your library or library system, you may be required to coordinate teen programs with those that are offered throughout the system. These programs, designed to attract teens to the library, are often viewed by the administration as excellent public relations tools. The pressure to plan and implement a system-wide program can be huge.

How can you as a single employee streamline these large programs? What follows are some suggestions to streamline the process and identify types of larger programs.

Reading Clubs

Teen librarians working in a stand-alone library, a mid-sized or large system are all expected to construct a summer reading program for young adults. There are even some libraries that sponsor both winter and summer reading programs. Reading clubs can be an annoyance to young adult librarians and I have heard many verbal frustrations being expressed about reading clubs. The goals of reading programs may be vague or have too much organized detail behind them, mostly depending on the past success or failure of the summer reading program. Still, some librarians approach the task of forming a reading club with enthusiasm, viewing them as another opportunity to bring teens into the library.

Usually the reading program orbits around a theme, which may be the same, or a spin-off, of the children's chosen theme. To simply adapt the children's theme may place a juvenile brand on your teen reading program, a characteristic that is sure to alienate young adult males from participating. A quick Internet search using the keywords "public library summer reading themes" resulted in many slogans, some teen friendly, and some not-so-teen friendly. I believe teen librarians would be working against themselves if forced to use such summer reading themes as "Wild about Books," "Books! A Treasure!" or "Paws, Claws, Scales, and Tales." I am a firm believer that teens need some degree of separation from the children's summer reading program, either completely or with an adaptation of the theme to make the theme edgier and more apt to attract teen readers. Work very hard to distinguish your teen reading club from that of the children's department, and allow teens in your library to develop a sense of self. They are young adults, not children or adults, and should have a framework in place at the library that helps carve out that identity. Being a "tacked on" part of a children's summer reading theme is counterproductive to teens achieving their own identities.

During their teen years, guys experiment with their limits and begin to challenge and break away from structure and authority. If a summer reading program has several levels of registration, has a complicated set of rules, or the incentives are kind of "cheesy," then guys will simply not participate.

Make certain that the framework of your reading program does not completely turn off teen males. Some tips on forming a reading club that attracts guys follow.

Make the Registration as Easy as Possible

Guys do not see the sense of filling out a lengthy form that hints of an emergency medical form required by schools. I have found that the easiest and most accessible way to register is for each book read: the teen fills out a slip of title, author, name, age, phone number, and rate the book on a number or star scale. Each time they fill out a slip, they essentially register.

Choose a Theme That Sounds Cool

During a summer reading program in a library system where I was employed, the children's theme was about journeys. I felt this did not translate too well into the teen world, so I adapted the theme for teens to be: Road Trip U.S.A. Not terribly original, but it sounded more teen friendly. Our graphics for our flyer featured lots of cars, which also drew teens by just a glance.

Incentives Can't Be Just Throw-Away Items

If a guy takes time to read a book, don't "reward" him with a pencil, or a sticker. Most teens would rather submit book entries for items they read to take a chance on winning a drawing. Only a few winners are picked each week, but that chance to win is more attractive than to be given some trite gift that makes you look like a goodie-two-shoes. Each week the reading club can have a different tone or theme, such as movie week (coupons to a movie theater), café week (a dollar off a coffee), book week (a gift card to a bookstore) and so on. Food works too. The prize for a week can be a gift certificate for a pizza, or simply be a 12-pack of soda.

Allow Guy-Type Books

All formats of reading should be allowed including graphic novels, nonfiction books, and fiction titles. Magazines are iffy choices and for some reading clubs, magazines do not qualify as a "book" read. On the other hand, many magazines contain more words than some photo album-type nonfiction books. Librarians like to quiz teens on what they liked about the book, and it is tough to get a solid answer about a graphic novel or a nonfiction book or magazine if the librarian is not familiar with these reading formats. Although this has not been the case in libraries where I have worked, I have been told of libraries that only allow fiction titles to be eligible for consideration to win. Only allowing fiction defeats the purpose of encouraging boys to participate in the reading club.

Teen Read Week

Another large system-wide program that is promoted by a large number of libraries is Teen Read Week. Promoted by YALSA (Young Adult Library Services Association), this national movement to recognize teen reading each year falls on the third week in October. YALSA chooses a theme and offers many programming suggestions through the YALSA Web page (see http://www.ala.org/yalsa).

The national theme has recently been voted by teens and for 2005 was Get Real!@your library and the theme for 2006 is Get Active@your library. These themes are open to broad interpretation and adaptations and should not alienate teen males.

My library invests the majority of the teen program budget to Teen Read Week and there is money to sponsor an author visit. When deciding on an author, ask yourself do you want guys to attend the author's talk, and if so, do the books this author writes have guy appeal? It doesn't matter if the author is female or male—the biggest concern is the writing. Does the author write about danger? Are there elements of action in the plot or are the author's stories heavy on romance and relationships?

During Teen Read Week of 2005, our library system suggested creating a system-wide program that would involve all 28 branches of the system. The young adult librarians came up with a program loosely based on the popularity of American Idol and using the Get Real!@your library theme (reality TV show). The teens sang a cappella in opening rounds at each branch, and winners advanced to a regional second round. From there, nine finalists were invited to compete for first prize. The program took months of planning and the logistics were detailed; but between participants and spectators, over 500 people attended the sessions. The good news? It was estimated that about a third of the participants were teen males and three of the nine finalists were guys. We were pleasantly surprised to have so much male participation for a singing competition. We concluded that opening the program up through all the branches encouraged the guys to join in, whereas if this program was conducted in a single location or on a smaller scale, guys would not be so eager to take part in the event.

PROGRAMS WITH GUY APPEAL

I have learned that guys often like to take charge of a program, *if* they can be involved from the beginning. Ownership is big to them. They like to see it through from planning to completion and want to be actively involved once the program begins. Girls I have worked with seemed to be more interested in planning and setting up, then stepping aside once the program began. This is just my personal observation; your girls and guys may have completely opposite characteristics.

However, if you notice this with your teens, use these guys. Introduce a concept or a framework of an idea and ask them to "fill in the blanks." For example, I sponsored an anime film festival that lasted from 10:00 A.M. to 4:00 P.M. on a Saturday. I facilitated the behind-the-scenes setup, securing the auditorium, and the necessary audio-visual equipment.

The guys were eager to do the legwork of recommending titles and find-ing out (by expertly digging in the Internet) how to contact the companies to ask for viewing permissions. They designed, at least a rough mock-up, of the publicity flyer. Since they knew the films they selected, they de-bated about the order of showing them. One young man became a leader by stepping forward and saying he wanted to introduce the whole event, filling the role of M.C. (Master of Ceremonies). I was amazed by the depth of their involvement.

Not to be outdone, the girls got involved with the setup displays on the day of the event and organized a raffle of some manga prizes. While the boys worked to get the overall project up and running, the girls focused on smaller, although equally important, details. Together their efforts made for a fine teen program. As an additional note, the boys' natural com-petitiveness came forward and they all wanted to be part of the "cool" jobs.

It is not always easy to find leaders, but they are there. Sometimes the leaders are quiet and competent, and in other cases the guy may be a loud and bragging type of person. Simply ask them if they can organize something. A good way to approach them for leadership tasks is to say, "I need your help and I think you are the guy that can get things done."

Some programs have a unisex appeal, and you may find yourself at a loss how to get the guys involved. For example, author visits run the risk of being detailed discussions about characters and the emotional turmoil woven throughout the story, which, as discussed, has more appeal to the girls. To take pressure of participation off the guys, offer them printed questions to ask the author. Have several of the boys organize and oversee an autograph table to keep the lines moving as the author signs. I am notorious for not remembering to have a camera ready for my programs. Ask the guys to be in charge of photography. They do like gadgets, especially things like digital cameras where they can see immediate results of their efforts; and this is one task they may take off your hands.

In my library system, we sometimes combine different aspects of programs. For example, we sponsored a teen summer reading finale and called it Teen Expo. We asked corporations to donate items that the teens could bid on with fake money. While that was going on, a Dance, Dance Revolution area was set up. The guys, although not that eager to take part in the dancing, were very interested in setting up the audiovisual equipment. To summarize, it is good to have a variety of things going on at any program. It is a good idea to outline the tasks necessary and figure out what should be done by the adults, what tasks are better suited to guys, and then which ones can be handled by the girls. Your framework does not have to be rigid, but having one is much better than hoping the guys show up and don't just hang around.

The following teen programs were sponsored by the libraries where I have worked as a young adult librarian. Some were constructed specifically to draw guys into the library and others just had guys show up, which was a pleasant surprise. Some drew over a 100 participants, and others had only 15 or so take part. Sometimes the majority of teens participating were male, others had a female majority, but also drew a strong male presence.

Chess for Success

This program involves an outside agency, in this case volunteers who organize a chess tournament from schools that sponsor chess clubs. It takes place in the library and features a double elimination tournament, chess tips from experts, and demonstrations of a master playing five teens simultaneously. A teen male's natural competitiveness may come forward, especially if the contestants are evenly matched. This is a program that almost requires preregistration. Include on the registration form a question about their skill level, that is, beginner, intermediate, or expert. While not exact, this will allow the teens to compete against someone near their own level and makes for more intriguing matches. Guys love to anticipate moves of their opponent and that cannot happen if one of the opponents is overwhelmed from the first move. Allow the guys to set up impromptu matches. Don't be so rigid and tied to a tournament schedule that you leave no room for their enthusiasm to continue to play on their own. Guys love this version of free form chess and the chance to do things on their own.

Halloween Party

On a whim, we threw a Halloween costume party, by decorating the meeting room with plastic Halloween ghosts, goblins, and pumpkins. What drew the guys was the "Write Your Own Epitaph" contest (using poster board cutouts in the shape of tombstones) and hiring a local theater make-up artist who created cuts, bruises, and other gross stuff on the guys. "Cheesy" black and white clips of old horror movies were shown on a big screen.

The second year I organized the Halloween party, I asked several guys for suggestions for some top music to try to time and play with the cool scenes of the horror movies. This became a task they really enjoyed. During a clip of a man turning into a werewolf from a film of the 1940s, the guys chose the song, *Kryptonite*, by 3 Doors Down. The phrase, "I watch the world float to the dark side of the moon," drew a huge laugh from the other teens. This simple and fun chore for the program really interested the young men, and they paid strict attention to detail. I would say that they had an initial experience of how to give a presentation, which can be labeled as a job skill.

Cartooning

Guys love to draw, so we asked local cartoonists to do a workshop on how they turned their teenage hobby into something of a career. Ask at your local comic bookstore if they have any contacts with cartoonists. There very well may be local people who, although not famous, can tell teens how to draw cartoon figures. I found these guys to be very generous with their time, and they did not talk down to the middle school teens. A potential problem may be that many teens today prefer drawing manga over American comics. In my own experience, it was fairly easy to locate artists who could demonstrate drawing American-style comics, but it took longer to uncover someone who could instruct how to draw manga. This may vary from region to region. Either way, a cartooning session is a productive program and one that the guys can leave with a created work; much like a make-it, take-it children's craft program. They may have been encouraged by an adult to pursue their hobby. I can say that in every library where I have worked, there have been teenaged guys isolated and in deep concentration about drawing comic characters, either their own creations or copying an illustration from a graphic novel. Use this interest to guide the guys into a loosely structured program.

Anime Club

Perhaps the reason so many guys come to my Anime club meetings is that I, the facilitator, am male, or maybe it is due to my showing an interest in a medium that interests them. For whatever reason, my anime club draws about 15 teens and usually there are only two or three girls. Future plans are being made for a kendo demonstration (the art of the Japanese warrior) and a cosplay (costume play) contest where teens dress up as their favorite Japanese comic book character. I have also arranged for a co-worker who is an adult librarian to conduct a brief lesson about learning Japanese language through manga. Another co-worker has presented tips on how to draw comics using the manga style. The lesson here is this; don't forget to survey your staff. They may surprise you about the hidden items of expertise they possess.

Although the atmosphere of the anime club meetings is very casual, participants are learning things that have direct connections to something they are very passionate about, manga and anime. Combining the huge interest in anime with a manga drawing demonstration makes for a great program. My dream program idea is to somehow have an anime producer or technician demonstrate how they create the anime videos. This, of course, requires much setup and probably a steep cost. But I can just imagine the wild interest that type of expertise being shared with teens would generate.

WWE Presentation

World Wrestling Entertainment has a promotion called Get R.E.A.L. (Respect, Education, Achievement, and Leadership), and offers promotions free of charge in the city where they are performing. The wrestlers arrive dressed in street clothes, not their costumes, and present a very positive message about education and the importance of reading. For many teens, these performers are professional athletes they can iden-tify from their access to cable TV. If your library meets the WWE re-quirements, the company will send you free posters to distribute to the teens. The boys really enjoy asking questions about which wrestler is their toughest opponent and which wrestler do they most fear. And of course, the guys always ask, "Are the matches fake?" The answer? The performers always say, "You can't fake hitting the mat." This opportu-nity to actually speak to a celebrity athlete is usually out of reach for most teens. Today the major stars of Major League Baseball, the Na-tional Basketball Association, or the National Football League are not allowed by agents or owners to spend significant amounts of time in the community. But professional wrestling sends a very positive mes-sage to teens, and the majority of the crowd at such a program is always male. More information about professional wrestling appearances can be found at the Web address: http://corporate.wwe.com/community/ getreal.jsp.

Poetry Slams

Guys seem to have a talent for free verse poetry. Each poetry group I have seen attracts several guys. They are talented, and like to per-form in front of other teens. Poetry groups are also sometimes formed by the school and they are looking for places to perform, which makes the public library a natural fit. In many school districts, any types of fine arts activities are after-school volunteer events. The teens are seek-ing a creative outlet for their talent and voices to be heard. Any poetry slam or even a poetry sharing is enhanced by including male voices and perspectives.

College Admissions Representative

If your library is near a college, that college probably has an outreach department. The job of that department is to recruit teens for that institu-tion. Recruiters like to speak to an after-school audience that often shows up in a public library. They may give tips on writing application essays, when and how often to take the standardized tests, and what the college experience is all about. Guys may not come to this type of program on their own, but perhaps it can be expanded to a college fair and open to both teens and parents of teens. Teens are often unsure of what they want to do if they go to college and it seems that they do not like to put things in order and end up completing college forms at the last minute. With a college recruiter coming to the library, which is something of a neutral ground between high school and the college itself, perhaps the young men will become more interested in the steps to pursue posthigh school education.

YWCA

Yes, this does say the YWCA. However, the program they presented was an educational outreach session on date rape. It was geared to girls, but guys sat in on it; and it was important information for them to hear. The YWCA has a set of educational outreach programs and they also enjoy the nice fit of speaking to the after-school crowd in public libraries. The local YWCA in my service area has an extensive packet of presentations, which they offer free of charge. They simply need an audience and are eager to visit the various branches in our system. Selecting by title, some of the programs that have guy appeal are:

- Alcohol, Cigarettes & Other Drugs
  The impact of drug use on their relationships, both with girl-friends and within their family, has a high appeal to teen males.
- Communication & Assertiveness Skills
  Guys are already bold, but this workshop explains the difference between assertiveness and aggression, and between positive and negative ways of communicating.
- Conflict Mastery/Anger Management
  The best component of this workshop for teenage boys is that they gain an understanding of and learn how to identify their own anger triggers.
- Sexually Transmitted Infections
  Teenage boys are beginning to explore their sexuality. It is an important service to provide a venue about learning the facts and prevention of STDs, HIV, and AIDS.
- Budgeting and Employment
  Guys are bombarded by advertisements pushing what they should wear, what electronic gear they need, and which is the coolest cell phone. All teenagers need to understand about the power of money, especially as they enter into their first job.

Search and Rescue Dogs

Animals and boys are a perfect match! An outside agency that trains the search dogs came and demonstrated how the animals respond to the commands. Middle school guys were fascinated on the dogs' ability to seek a person simply by smell.

To further engage teen males in programs, observe the nonfiction books that the guys read in your library. You might find out that paintball, NASCAR, professional wrestling, photography, or hot-rods are what they are interested in learning more about. I've found in my experience that teen guys come to programs that feature an outside presenter rather than the librarian trying to drive the program. This is just my experience and your situation may be different. But always be alert to any community organization that wants to promote their services. Often they are free or relatively inexpensive and love the fact that the library can gather an audience for them.

TEEN ADVISORY BOARDS

Teen Advisory Boards have long been touted as an ideal method of drawing teens to the library and offering them empowerment over what can happen in the teen section of the library. Teen Advisory Boards go by many different sets of acronyms, but what I use is the phrase Teen Advisory Board or TAB. There are many articles and books published about the logistics of forming an advisory board. There are also many statements from both teens and adults justifying the purpose and importance of using an advisory board to connect with teens. Are they worthwhile? Are they worth the librarian's effort? Do they make a difference? In her book, *Library Teen Advisory Boards*, Diane Tuccillo states, "If done correctly with committed advisors, the answers are a resounding yes!" (Tuccillo 2005).

Although most librarians understand the importance of having advisory boards, what often is overlooked is how to engage teen males to become part of one. Another concern is, if they do participate, how to keep them interested in coming back?

Including Guys on the Teen Advisory Board

There are two challenges that commonly come up when librarians try to include guys in any program or to get them involved to be part of a teen advisory board. One situation could be described as follows. There is a large after-school crowd that visits the library and this crowd includes a significant number of teen boys. How do you determine which guys may be interested in the advisory board, get them off of the floor, away from their buddies, and into a productive meeting? The second challenge is when guys rarely, if ever, visit the library and the teen librarian's contact with teens is mostly with girls. What follows are some brainstormed strategies on how to attract guys to a teen advisory board (and keep them coming back!).

The Structure and Atmosphere of the Teen Advisory Board Meeting

Before distributing any recruiting publicity, put it under a review and ask yourself, "Is it too feminine in appearance?" Evaluate the color of the paper (Is it pink or a soft pastel?). What font was chosen? Does it have a bold impact or a soft suggestion? What clip art was used? Are the figures female, male, or a balance of both? Teens make snap judgments on covers of books and will do the same quick acceptance or shun of a flyer-based on their overall first impression.

Once inside the meeting room, what do the teens see? Tablecloths? Cute plates? Ribbons? Glitter and sparkles? I am not suggesting making the atmosphere so bland it seems like a jail cell, but the goal is to welcome guys and make them feel comfortable, not put them on edge.

The meeting should have an agenda, but it should not be so regimented that guys feel like this is an extension of school. The first item on my agenda is always 5 to 10 minutes of free talk during which I encourage the teens to share what cool things are happening at their schools. (I have always worked in a system that draws from different schools). I have found that teens, both boys and girls, like to compare activities from sports, drama club, to band and how these things differ from school to school.

Take the Pre-Meeting Organization upon Yourself

Teens, especially boys, balk if they sense that they are responsible for doing everything. Once the meeting starts, let them take it where it will go within the structure of your agenda. The meeting should accomplish goals that are clearly stated, not just turn into a gab session. I believe that deep down, guys want a linear path to a goal and won't tolerate many digressions into chitchat. As the librarian and group facilitator, you need to bring the groups back when the teens waiver from the agenda. The good phrase to use is, "OK that was fun, now back to business." The guys and girls will respect you for being strong.

When to Schedule the Meetings

In today's world, a teenager's time is booked pretty solid with school, extracurricular activities, and jobs. They also do not usually have a parent driving them to these events and may have transportation issues. Scheduling a teen advisory board meeting is tricky. There seems to be no single perfect day or time. In my experience, scheduling a meeting on any weekday never seemed to please the entire group. Once a day was suggested, only a handful here and there would agree to that day. Of course, the majority said that day would not be good for them.

To enlist guys in a teen advisory board meeting, choosing the right day and time is important. I know some librarians have had success with the meetings held after school, but I have not. I tried them at night, around 7:00 P.M. but only a handful of teens showed up and they were girls, the super-teen types who would have adjusted their schedules to any time I suggested. I heard guys tell me they were busy after school with sports, or band, or drama. That pushed back their study and free times and they did not want to come to the library at night and return home possibly after 9:00 P.M.

The solution that worked for me was Saturday. I work alternating Saturdays (as do most teen librarians whom I know). I labeled the teen advisory board meeting a "working lunch" and we met at noon for about an hour. This time seemed to work out for most people, and we had fairly consistent attendance. The guys did not have to give up their social prime time and they became valuable contributors to the group.

Food Is a Must

Whether your teen advisory board meetings are planned for after school, in the evening or on a Saturday, there is one thing you can count on—teens are hungry. Be sure to have snacks and drinks on hand, especially for the guys. Pizza is good, but can be expensive, and some libraries do not reimburse the librarians for food. What surprised me was that both the guys and the girls seemed to enjoy the more affordable offering of milk (or a juice drink) and cookies. So that became the standard of our meetings. This food choice meant less clean up, and nobody looked stupid with strings of cheese hanging out of their mouths. (Remember, guys do not want to appear weak or foolish in front of anyone; and their eating habits, if mocked by the girls, might cause them not to return to any meetings.) It seems to be a small thing but choosing the "right" food is almost a necessity and could be the hook that gets them to the meeting.

Avoid Being Overbearing

The last thing a teenage guy wants to deal with on his own time is a morphed form of his parents or classroom teachers. Be careful not to be the all-controlling adult in the room. Ask for their opinions and do not be afraid to suggest an activity that you know nothing about. Sometimes it is good to be the dumbest person in the room. During my anime club meetings, the teens begin to chat about directors, artwork, how a certain series is a rip-off of a previous series and so on. I pretended to know nothing (sometimes not so much of a pretend), and asked questions about what I should look for in the DVDs we view. This led to some great conversations about the artwork of classic anime films versus cheap imitations. Understand that teens may have superior knowledge of a topic over you. Online gaming, anime, and Web site construction are examples of topics that chances are, teens know more about than adults. Park your ego and listen.

When the Teens (or Guys) Ask, "What's In It for Me?"

Too often a teen advisory board can turn into something of a burden for the teens. Perhaps they signed up to fulfill community service hours. Maybe they were searching for an item to fill-in-the-blank on a college application. But if you place restrictive rules and procedures on the teens, they just may not return for a second meeting. This is especially true of teen males. They want to know the bottom line, or what they will receive for contributing their free time. The answer? I mention early and often in teen advisory board meetings that if they put in their time and contribute, then I would be more than happy to write a one-page reference for them for a job or college application. Many teens have taken me up on this, and they appreciate being viewed as more than anonymous volunteers. Another method to promote your teen advisory board is to submit articles about activities they have accomplished. The articles can appear in your library newsletter, local newspapers, regional or statewide reports, or even national publications.

Call It Something Else

To many teenage guys, the phrase teen advisory board, or similar phrases, sounds too much like student council work. They need to know if it is going to be interesting, fun, or a grinding, labor-intensive hour out of their life. You don't have to call your group a name that suggests work. The idea is to gain feedback from teens about what is cool, or what could be a cool thing, in the library. In my library system, several young adult librarians have decided to seize any opportunity to talk to teens about what should the library do to enhance teen services. Thus we have groups that meet regularly such as anime clubs, a Snack and Yak club, and a Teen Zone Crew. All are accomplishing the goal of listening to teens, but the groups do not smack of faceless volunteerism. This keeps both the males and females coming back to the next scheduled meeting. A success story came about after 2 years of anime meetings. One young man said, "This is okay and all, but can't we do other things?" Thus a teen advisory board of sorts was formed with the teens being the initial catalyst. Let me pass on this advice. I asked the teens what they wanted to call the group, for example, a teen advisory board, or TAB. I was quickly told, "We'd never come to anything named that." Thus, they came up with the label of L.B.E. (Library, Books, Entertainment) Teens with Ideas. They believe this sounds much edgier and "cool." I have to agree.

While there are no sure-fire methods of attracting guys to your teen advisory board meeting, there are things you can evaluate to determine if your existing method of attracting teens does in fact appeal to guys as well as teen girls. The only must-do item for you, the teen librarian, to accomplish is to plan the meeting. Of course, guys will test the waters, but if there is some nonoverbearing structure in place and they feel the meeting is not a waste of their time, then maybe, just maybe, they will become contributing members of the teen advisory board.

REFERENCES

Chelton, Mary K. *Excellence in Library Services to Young Adults. The Nation's Top Programs.* 2nd edition. Chicago, IL: American Library Association, 1997.

Honnold, RoseMary. *101 + Teen Programs That Work.* New York: Neal-Schuman Publishers, Inc., 2003.

Search Institute, 2002. "Development Assets: An Overview" [online]. Available at http://www.search-institute.org/assets/ [2006, March 5].

Tuccillo, Diane P. *Library Teen Advisory Groups.* Lanham, MD: VOYA Books, 2005.

Chapter 7

SCHOOL VISITS AND BOOKTALKS

Librarians and library administrators lament that, despite a tremendous effort to counteract the trend, it is becoming increasingly difficult to bring patrons into the library. In many library systems, declining circulation figures point to the reality that fewer people use library services. One of the tasks expected of teen librarians is to encourage teens to come to the library and use the materials the library offers. This is a tough task and not always possible, but the minimum goal is to at least inform the teens of what services and materials are available to them in the library. One of the best ways to do that is to meet the teens on their own turf.

Young people entering their teenage years begin to test boundaries and venture out into a larger world. They begin to travel, usually in groups, to places that appeal to them such as malls, bookstores, coffee shops, or libraries. As stated in earlier chapters, a library, simply because of the overall atmosphere of the building or the attitude of the employees, may not attract teens. Conversely, some libraries take astounding measures to make the teen area of the library welcoming to teens. Regardless of your library's approach to teens, remember, nobody can force a teen to come to the library. For a variety of reasons, teen males in particular may be unsure or unwilling to pass through the front doors of a library. If the teens, and for this book's purpose teen males, are not inside your library building, what course of action can you take?

The answer is to go to places where there are teens. In theory, outreach services for teens can be sent anywhere teens happen to be at that moment. It can be an informal and impromptu give-and-take at a bookstore in the manga section where you ask a teenager what are his, or her, favorite series. Outreach services can also happen at an after-school recreational center for younger teens who still fall under the latchkey label. Connecting with teens can even happen in a youth development center with incarcerated teens.

Successful outreach services depend on communication, organization, and coordinated preplanning with adults who sponsor these areas where teens are. Do this before actually planning the framework of the outreach action. A teen librarian who shows up unannounced to a teen center, a jail or a coffeehouse to spread the word of great teen books and services may be viewed with raised eyebrows by both teens and adults.

CONNECTING WITH SCHOOLS

A place where teens are guaranteed to congregate in large numbers, an establishment that has a goal of promoting literacy, and an institution where the adults appreciate any services you can offer, is a school—and more specifically, a school library. There are many reasons why outreach services from a public library to school libraries make sense. These outreach services may benefit both types of libraries that quite possibly serve the same teen population.

Budget Crunches Effect Both Public and School Libraries

If the library budget has been drastically cut, decisions are made as to what is essential to keep the library functional. Neither schools nor public libraries ever purchase all the materials available to them each year. School libraries sometimes only purchase items requested by teachers under the assurance the materials will be definitely used in the classroom. Sometimes, school library budgets are so miniscule there are only enough dollars to purchase news magazines for research, a subscription to a local newspaper and a few repair supplies to keep the necessary books circulating. Oddly enough (and frustrating to school librarians), the school may have a separate hardware budget, or a government grant, which allows several, if not many, computers to be purchased for the library. I've witnessed bizarre library versions of a "Tale of Two Sections" where up-to-date computers are booted up and are in constant use by many teens. On the other side of the same room are bookshelves holding a book collection that has not been weeded in years. To further emphasize the bizarre situation, the book collection may contain cast-off titles obtained from public library book sales.

On the other hand, public libraries experiencing budget cuts sometimes, by arbitrarily made decisions, stop buying books that support the local school curriculum. Many public libraries' funding decisions are based on circulation numbers; and when money is tight, teen librarians selectively purchase items that have a high chance of circulating. So, money problems cause cuts in materials that harm teens. If the two libraries serving the teen population somehow collaborate, then the teens have a better opportunity to have their library needs met.

The School Library Offers Fewer Hours of Access Than the Public Library

School libraries do the best they can to stay open throughout the school day. Librarians committed to services often are on duty before school actually opens to allow a teen to check out a book just before homeroom. Many stay open during lunchtime to allow teens a place to finish homework or just be comfortable (which ends up resembling the atmosphere in a public libraries' teen area).

Beyond that, it has to be rare for a school library to be open on weekends or at night during the week. Public libraries, on the other hand, have several peak moments of patron rushes. During the morning hours, adults frequent the library to select books, scan the stock reports, or read an out-of-town newspaper. But after school, the focus in most libraries shifts to teens entering the building. They are there to accomplish a homework assignment, or to log on to computers to get their Internet fix or to find the latest and greatest title.

Just as neither type of library can provide all the print materials needed by the teens, neither library can provide all of the service hours that teens need. In Ohio, the after-hours online help service at night called Know-It-Now draws far more teens than adults, thus reinforcing the fact that teens need to use the library. Teens want to use the library services. It just might not be during the hours posted on the front door.

There Are Guys in the Schools

Unless the school is designated an all-girls school, there will be teen males in the school building; and meeting them on their own turf is a great way to connect with guys. Visiting a school places the teen librarian in the guy's home environment and eliminates the possibility of guys "acting out" and being disruptive. Many male teens that I talk to state that they "never" go to either the public or school library. A classroom visit from the teen librarian from the public library might be viewed as a welcome relief to the steady stream of assignments. Also, teens are usually receptive to a new voice in their environment. The advantage public librarians have is that their visits are not seen as the same old, same old, school drudgery. Thus, there is a good chance to connect with teen males, just by your entering the school building.

The Teachers Know the Students

It is often frustrating for me, employed at a large public library system, to talk to teens, perhaps catch their names and recommend books I think they will like, and then not see them for several weeks. In classrooms, teachers see the same teens every day; they know something about them and their personalities. This is a big first step for readers' advisory. During booktalks, I have had teachers chime in with comments such as, "Oh, Jimmy, I know you would like this book."

Too often public library teen librarians do not have a chance to really get to know their patrons. This of course depends on the size of the library and how often the teens come back. I believe due to the lesser number of teen patrons, a smaller library can be far more successful in connecting teens to books, but on the other hand, the smaller budget may lead to the library having a limited selection of titles. A school teacher or school librarian may have great insight into what a teen male likes to read, but has no way to actually connect that guy to a book. When a public librarian can fill this void during a school visit, he or she performs very important work of hooking boys (and girls) to books. To sum it up, a school has the guaranteed audience and the public library most likely has the materials. Can they connect with each other? How should a school visit be conducted?

THE SCHOOL VISIT—A GAME PLAN

For some reason, there seems to be no middle ground (at least in the libraries where I have worked) for a connection between the schools and the public library. In some cases, the relationship has been very positive. As a teen librarian, I was often invited to present booktalks to English classes. In contrast, some schools and public libraries, have little or no connection. I've often heard from public librarians that those schools are just "messed up," and it is too hard to contact anyone inside the school.

Having always worked in a library system that served several school districts and buildings, I have noticed that the receptiveness varies from school to school. Some schools invite me in monthly, or twice during a 9-week period, and other schools (at a comparable distance from the public library facility) never took the steps to contact me for a visit. Even your best proactive efforts to connect to schools may fail. Some teachers and school administrators simply adapt a bunker mentality. They are very reluctant for any outsider to interrupt their school day or invade their territory.

Your first step is to let the school people know who you are. A one-page cover letter on the public library's letterhead explaining who you are, how long you have been a teen librarian, and your desire to provide services to the school (and an outline of what those services are) is a great way for you to lay the first plank of a bridge to the schools.

Mail copies of your letter to the principal of the school, the head of the English department, and the school media specialist. If there is no head of the English department, a phone call to the secretary can give you the names of teachers. A direct mailing is only effective if the right people get the mailing.

Hint: The two times a school is flooded with mail is at the end of school in June and the beginning of school in August. Sadly, if mailed during these peak times, there is a chance your letter will be tossed into the trash with a flood of junk mail. Time your mailing 2 weeks after the start of school. This may seem as working against the desire to provide a back-to-school presence, but in my experience it works. For the first 2 weeks of school, the staff does not seem to want any interruptions to the flow of the school day. Planning a back-to-school program at the public library may be a better option than asking to enter the school building at this key transition period.

Another way to connect with the schools is to attend any system or countywide library function. Many school districts have a librarians' group that meets monthly to discuss online services, central ordering through a county office, or to trends in the school library field. There are also professional workshops held locally or regionally where you can make connections.

Plan ahead what items you want to include in the visit, from promotional materials to library sign-up sheets to the types of books. I have begun e-mailing the teacher a list of books I will bring to the school, so the teacher can make copies of the list for each student. This also allows the teacher, or school librarian, to buy into the content of the presentation. They may look over the booktalk titles to check the list against their own collection. This is more effective than bringing multiple copies of the list, when the teacher and students both see the list for the first time. It is a huge reward upon returning to the public library to see a student with your list in hand asking where he or she can find a certain book!

An often overlooked step in preparation for a booktalk at school is to ask the teacher or media specialist what books have been required reading for the teens. This information gives you a starting point with the types of books the teens have been reading. This also provides a base knowledge about the reading abilities for the students.

With today's extensive testing in schools, there is often little time for a teacher to abandon his or her lesson plans for a class period to hear book-talks and book promotions from the public library. Don't be discouraged—ask to set up a display table during lunchtime. Several young adult library friends have done this exact thing and have reported back great experiences. Apparently, the teens are receptive because the connection is not in a classroom or the public library, but sort of a halfway point. I have always been lucky enough to have the teachers invite me into their classrooms. But other friends who are teen librarians report a great success during the lunch hours. I do take part in a lunchtime book discussion at a local high school, and have found it is a great way to meet the teens on their turf. However, remember that lunch periods are short, so do not expect to go into great detail about any library or book topic during this time.

How much time should you take to perform this outreach service? This is the place for a few comments about time spent at the schools. Be aware that teen outreach to the schools is different than a children's visit. I've observed children's librarians departing to visit several schools in the morning to promote library card signups or summer reading. They tell me that the classroom teachers only allow 20 minutes for their talk, so in one morning they may visit several classrooms in a variety of schools.

Teachers in a secondary school play by a different set of rules. An elementary classroom teacher doesn't want a total distraction and undergo the work of regaining the focus of the students. On the other hand, a middle school or high school teacher wants the teen librarian to use the whole period and then simply send the class on to their next subject when the bell rings. Enter the school with enough material to be prepared to speak for 45 minutes. Warning: Some schools have adapted a block scheduling system where the periods are 90 minutes long. That is way too long to hold the teens' attention; and the teacher should realize that this time needs to be split up to be most beneficial for all parties concerned.

During the beginning of the period, explain the importance of a library card, or mention any upcoming library programming that might appeal to the teens. Distribute program flyers if you have them. After these promotional announcements, begin a series of booktalks. Come prepared with samples of books from all genres, including nonfiction and graphic novels. Of course, remember to include titles from all formats and genres that are boy-friendly. After all, during a school visit, it is a sure bet boys will be there. One important hint, especially if visiting a school for the first time, ask in advance what types of books, or specific titles, the teacher or school does not want presented. (Schools operate under a different set of rules than public libraries, and that is something you need to keep in mind.)

Plan to speak for the whole class period, and prepare to present to several different periods in a row. Being at a school for a full half of a day may disrupt your other professional duties, especially if your teen services job is combined with another library department. Filling in extra time on front desk duty for a teen librarian who is out of the building can ruffle an adult service librarian's feathers. Be sure to give advance warning of when your school visit is scheduled. Unfortunately, some schools may not give you enough advance notice. If your department supervisor needs a month advance notice to formulate the desk schedule, be sure to include that information in the letter you send.

Speaking to four or more classes in a row can be exhausting, but it is the best way to connect with a large number of teens. I can't think of any sure-fire programs that will attract 120 to 150 teens, but that many can easily be reached through a school visit during a morning of classes.

Don't be surprised if other classes ask to "sit in" on the talk. I have had up to three classes enter the library to hear booktalks. It gets crowded and the teens' attention span may wander if the room becomes too crowded. Ideally, the best number to present to at a school visit in one class period is between 25 and 35 students.

During any outreach function, keep in mind that you are representing the public library. Since the September 11 terrorist attacks, schools have adopted many procedures for visitors to the school. The librarian should arrive early enough to go through these procedures and still be on time to set up for the presentation. Procedures vary. I have been told by some office workers to simply "take a left and go down the hall." Other schools require a sign-in sheet and presentation of a photo ID. A school ID is then attached on your shirt or sweater. Whatever the procedure the school has in place, abide by it, and do as they ask, even if it seems to be unnecessary. Remember if you unwittingly cause a procedure problem, it reflects poorly on the public library to all the school employees.

Of course, many things can go wrong during a school visit. The fire alarm might go off and everyone must exit the building. The PA system might begin to ask for students to report to the office and drown out your presentation. The teachers may be very interested and interrupt too much; or they may be totally disinterested and withdraw from the presentation to grade papers. Teens may act out or use the time as a gossip session. However, for me, school visits are very rewarding. I always feel I have connected with teens in a way that is more effective than an in-house library program. Following a successful school visit, if teens journey to and enter the public library, it is because they heard something from you that sparked their interest. This moment of professional joy can be marked down as a definite win-win situation.

BOOKTALKING AT SCHOOLS—MAKE IT GUY-FRIENDLY

Booktalks can be considered a program, and this quite probably is one of the cheapest programs you can present. That is not to say it is an easy program to pull together. To present a booktalk that engages both the males and females of the audience, prepare to present selected titles from a wide range of genres such as fantasy, horror, historical fiction, realistic fiction, and so on. This means lots of advance reading to familiarize yourself with the titles. Keep a rotation of the titles to remain fresh. We all have our favorite books and our no-fail booktalks, but teens want what is brand new. Remember, they are in tune with the Internet and may already know of books being released that very month.

There are many ways to conduct booktalks, from acting out the scenes, engaging a teen audience member for a short reader's theater skit, or using props. My advice is to be honest and straightforward rather than try to wow the teens. Do you as a teen librarian want to be the focus of the booktalk, or let the book sell itself? Props can be very helpful, but consider how easy or difficult it will be to transport the material to a school.

When presenting new titles to an adult audience at a workshop, I utilize a Microsoft Powerpoint slide show presentation, which shows the covers of the books on the screen. I have tried this same technique for booktalking to teens and the time-consuming hassle of setting up the electronic components was huge. Teens would rather see the actual books than an electronic version of the covers, which makes it feel like a lecture rather than an interactive conversation.

1. There is no absolutely 100 percent effective way to present a booktalk, but the most important result is to share books with teens through the personal contact way. This is best accomplished by going to the school and giving a booktalk.

2. Be yourself. Teens have a built-in meter for dishonesty that works with astounding speed and is very accurate. They will shut down if they feel you are not being truthful of how you really feel about the books.

3. Try to become familiar with both middle school and high school books and proficient at presenting to both grade levels. There is a huge difference between just the 24 months separating 7th grade and 9th grade.

4. Only booktalk books you have actually read and you as a reader enjoyed. If you are indifferent to the book, teens will pick up on that negative attitude.

5. Before launching into the meat of the booktalk, mention the title and author and also comment on the cover art. Also mention any other popular or recent titles written by that author.

6. Don't ever give away the ending of a scene, or the whole book. Think of it as a teaser, much like a movie preview of upcoming movies that are shown in theaters. You ideally want the teens to become interested in the book, the characters, and the conflict, and for guys, any danger that will occur.

7. Stand, don't sit, while presenting a book to a group of teens. Let your enthusiasm for the book come forth.

8. Know your audience (if possible) beforehand. Ethnic makeup? Religious makeup? More boys than girls? Remedial or advanced students? Reluctant or avid readers?

9. Bring a variety of books and some can be just show and tell. Include the browsing type of nonfiction, graphic novels, magazines, and audiobooks.

10. Ask for a table to set the books on and display the cover artwork. In a pinch, a chalkboard tray or windowsill can be used to stand up the books and display the front covers. Ask the teens which ones they would like to know more about just by the appearance of the title and the cover. This icebreaking question engages the audience.

Ten Concepts about Booktalks

Types of Booktalks

There are many styles of booktalks. Which you use depends in part on your own taste and comfort. However, I recommend employing several different styles, mixing them up so students don't get bored with a particular approach. In my opinion, there really is no right way or wrong way to present books to a teen audience. What is more important is that you willingly approach teens and present the power of a book to them in a brief and concise way.

Narrative

Give a summary of the book. Try to include the who, what, when, where, and why about the book and also describe the character's main conflict in the story. Try to keep the narrative under a 3-minute time limit. I have found it helpful to not worry too much about the character's name, but to include the character's age in your narrative. Teens want to read about someone 1 or 2 years older than them. If the character is younger, chances are they will not be too interested in the story, no matter how creative a booktalk you present.

Synopsis

Read a short section (less than 45 seconds) of the book to set a tense scene, illustrate the character's personality or the conflict he or she is undergoing. Use a Post-it note or bookmark at the passage to be read beforehand. If you even take as little as 30 seconds to find the section, teens will mentally drift away from you. Post-it notes can also be cheats to jot down character's names, the name of the town as a setting, etc.

First Person Narrative

Present the booktalk as if you were the character telling what is happening so far and how you feel about what might happen to you later in the story. (It is helpful to know your audience and they know who you are before attempting this acting job—teens can be very, very cruel). If you feel comfortable with the teens, print out the first person narrative, ask for anyone with acting ability, and have them read what happens to the character in the book. Do some coaching about reading with the emotion the character is feeling such as sorrow, excitement, or anger. This teen involvement breaks up the booktalk session by having the audience hear another voice.

First Sentence

Sometimes just reading the first sentence is a very effective booktalk, as it delineates the character and conflict and may also introduce other characters in just one sentence. For example, in the 2006 book, *Samurai Shortstop* (Gratz, Alan. New York: Dial Books, 2006), this stunner of a first sentence will almost certainly grab teenage boys' attention. "Toyo watched carefully as his uncle prepared to kill himself."

More Types of Books to Booktalk

I like to hook books to popular culture or news items. The book *Phineas Gage: A Gruesome but True Story about Brain Science* (Fleischman, John. Boston, MA: Houghton Mifflin, 2002.) relates the story of a railroad man of the 1800s who has an iron rod driven through his skull by a dynamite explosion. The cover shows his skull with the hole where the rod exited. Mr. Gage actually received a crude lobotomy. To hook this book to the present day, a quick search of the Internet reveals the Darwin Awards (http://www.darwinawards.com. There is also a print version of the Darwin Awards). To hook the Darwin Awards to *Phineas Gage*, inform the teens of the article about a roofer in Australia who playfully shot himself in the head with a nail gun. For a week he did not realize he had a nail driven into his brain and wondered why he was getting so many headaches. Teenage guys, especially middle school guys, love these types of stories that involve the absurd and gross.

Books that have been made into movies are good hooks for boys. This is especially true if the teacher or media specialist allows the teen librarian to booktalk graphic novels. Guys like to be introduced (if they already don't know of them) to the print versions of Spiderman, Hellboy, the Fantastic Four, the X-Men, and so on. Several manga titles such as Full Metal Alchemist, Hellsing, and Inu-Yasha, while not shown in theaters, have been adapted into half-hour episodes that are shown on television or online. In areas of the country where manga rules, the teens might enthusiastically tell you about the plots, characters, conflicts, and magical powers woven throughout the series.

Many booktalkers practice their talk over and over and plan an order to the books presented, so that one book links to the next by similar plots, characters, or author. Other booktalking professionals like to write out their booktalks. I never do. I like to keep an eye on the audience and if the talk does not grab them and I am reading instantly bored body language, I can wrap up that book quickly and move on to the next one. I personally do not want to be tied to a script. But, as stated earlier in this chapter, I believe there is no completely right or wrong way to perform a booktalk.

The concept of transitioning from one book to the next smoothly is a talent. You need to know a variety of books and know them well enough that you can illustrate a common thread between the titles. To expand the thinking of connecting different titles, a great way to engage the guys in the class is to offer a nonfiction book on the topic tying in the plot of a fiction title. Guys love the spy action in the Alex Rider Series by Anthony Horowitz. A great nonfiction book to further land the hook is *Ultimate Spy* (Melton, H. Keith. New York: DK Publishing, 2002.), a title filled with photographs of all kinds of spy gear.

Connecting with Middle School Boys through Booktalks

Middle school boys are caught in the in-between area of wanting to be introduced to edgier topics and books, but still clinging to juvenile types of activities and reading. To interest this age of boys, introduce books with plenty of action, even those bordering on the absurd. Nonfiction books should have lots of illustrations, but about specific things rather than big concepts that provoke deep thought. Examples for nonfiction can be *The Worst-Case Scenario Survival Handbook* (Piven, Joshua and Borgenicht, David. San Francisco, CA: Chronicle Books, 1999) or *Odd Jobs: Portraits of Unusual Occupations* (Nancy Rica. Berkeley, CA: Ten Speed Press, 2002). Almost a sure hit for boys of this age are the annual additions to the *Ripley's Believe or Not* series, which is a bit more twisted than the *Guinness Book of World Records*.

These guys usually want none of that icky romance stuff. If there are girls in their life, they may be more like buddies. Fiction series with titles that are solid choices for action and also some sort of relationship with a female are *The Hungry City Chronicles* by Philip Reeve, *Sleeper Conspiracy* series by Tom Sniegoski, and the *Artemis Fowl* series by Eoin Colfer. If possible, take along to your booktalk some magazines that are very visual such as *Mad* magazine, *GamePro*, and *NewType*.

Connecting with High School Boys through Booktalks

High school boys are really into being independent and being self-sufficient. Their reading tastes for nonfiction are the readable books laced with illustrations but about topics on a bigger scale like war, professional sports, or motorcycles, or cars. A booktalk about memoirs will be accepted if they have a cool factor, such as a music artist or a sports figure with a sensationalized private life (Kurt Cobain, Tupac, Biggie Smalls, or Kobe Bryant). In my experience, high school boys like to be introduced to, and read about, realistic things happening outside of their own environment.

Nonfiction can include *Skateboarding is Not a Crime: 50 Years of Street Culture* (Davis, James. Buffalo, NY: Firefly Books, 2004), or *Streetball: All the Ballers, Moves, Slams and Shine* (Palmer, Chris. New York: HarperResource, 2004). To hook them to fiction, the novel has to have a certain amount of suspense and action. *Miracle's Boys* (Woodson, Jacqueline. New York: G. P. Putnam's Sons, 2000), *Dark Angel* (Klass, David. New York: Farrar, Straus and Giroux, 2005) and *You Don't Know Me* (Klass, David. New York: Frances Foster Books, 2001) are titles I have booktalked with very positive reactions from high school boys.

Bring along copies of *Vibe* magazine, *ESPN the Magazine*, and *Slam* magazine to further attract boys who may not want to tackle a hardback book.

Connecting with the Avid Teen Male Readers through Booktalks

Teen males who are avid readers want to be challenged mentally by books they read. They want to branch into more serious literature that also has some degree of action and features danger, but at the same time introduces character introspection. Many avid teen males are fans of fantasy or anything that hints of themes introduced by Tolkien. Some other title suggestions are *Johnny Got His Gun* (Trumbo, Dalton. New York: J. B. Lippincott, 1939), *Feed* (Anderson, M. T. Cambridge, MA: Candlewick Press, 2002), *Amaryllis* (Crist-Evans, Craig. New York: Clarkson Potter, 2002), *Full Tilt* (Shusterman, Neal. New York: Simon & Schuster, 2003), and *Stuck in Neutral* (Trueman, Terry. New York: HarperCollins Publishers, 2000).

Nonfiction should cover events and issues that occur worldwide. Introduce teens to the book *Black Hawk Down* (Bowden, Mark. New York: Atlantic Monthly Press, 1999), and inform them that the movie is very different than the book. Give a booktalk about soldiers just out of their teens and their feelings about being at war. An excellent choice is *Generation Kill: Devil Dogs, Iceman, Captain America and the New Face of American War* (Wright, Evan. New York: G. P. Putnam's Sons, 2004).

For an offbeat magazine that challenges an avid reader, provide a brief introduction to *Mental Floss*, a magazine that includes fascinating trivia about things we just think we know something about.

Great Books That Connect with Male Readers through Booktalks

Acceleration (McNamee, Graham. New York: Wendy Lamb Books, 2003).

The narrative of 17-year-old Duncan discovering the diary of a serial killer and then having the man ask for the notebook at the lost and found counter. Duncan's obsession with tracking down the would-be murderer and the subsequent suspense completely engages male readers. A great cliffhanger is to stop the narration just when Duncan goes down to the killer's basement . . .

Jade Green: A Ghost Story (Naylor, Phyllis Reynolds. New York: Atheneum, 1999).

Tell the middle school guys about the ghost who is bothering Judith Sparrow, and then one night materializes as a severed hand that crawls along the floor and disappears . . . under her bed. A great ghost story book for middle school boys.

Cirque du Freak (Shan, Darren. Boston, MA: Little, Brown, 2001).

The series includes many titles, but a seventh-grade boy might have not yet been introduced to any of the books. Booktalk all the gross stuff. Mention the huge spider, a freaky vampire, saving your friend from certain death, the deal made with the vampire and oh yeah, how the character gets buried alive. Great scenes with high guy appeal occur throughout the entire series.

Playing in Traffic (Giles, Gail. Brookfield, CT: Roaring Brook, 2004).

There is danger in this book in the form of Skye, a goth girl who comes on strong to Matt, a guy who just wants to drift through school. Read the section where Skye greets Matt at his locker and slowly traces her index finger down his cheek and whispers to him that he "might be the one." The guys will wish they would be the one!

Tears of a Tiger (Draper, Sharon. New York: Aladdin Paperbacks, 1994).

The consequences of a poor decision about driving drunk leading to the horrible death of a friend will hit home very hard with teen boys on the verge of getting their driver's license. Many boys say this book is just like things that happen out in the real world.

Black and White (Volponi, Paul. New York: Viking, 2005).

Guys will be riveted while listening to a brief summary of events causing two friends to risk their promising futures by doing armed robberies. End the booktalk with the tease, "One of them is going to jail."

In the Paint: Tattoos of the NBA and the Stories Behind Them (Gottlieb, Andrew. New York: Hyperion, 2003).

This can almost be a silent booktalk. Just prop the book up so the guys can see the cover and just mention that Allen Iverson has around 20 tattoos. Allow 5 minutes at the end of the period to browse the books and I wager the guys will open *Tattoos of the NBA* and find out more about the players' body art.

Amazonia (Rollins, James. New York: Morrow, 2002).

If the criteria for a book to be a teen novel are that it must have teen characters and involve teen issues, then *Amazonia* is not a teen novel. But reading a thrill-a-page book about a group of men struggling through the Amazon jungle fighting off vicious panthers, amphibious piranha, and crocodiles that are bigger than their boats has a great guy appeal. During the booktalk, I describe reading this title almost like being caught inside a video game where you have to battle your way out of danger.

Revenge of the Witch: The Last Apprentice (Delaney, Joseph. New York: Greenwillow Books, 2005).

At first glance this book seems like a fairy tale as it describes Thomas Ward, the seventh son of a seventh son. The cover does hint about danger showing a hooded figure striding through a graveyard with a lantern. However, a booktalk suggesting how dumb Thomas is when he allows the witch to escape and he must risk his life to recapture her will have boys rushing to check out the book.

Now, a word about teens checking out books following a successful booktalk. In the libraries I have worked in, there was no way to have an instant checkout at the school following a booktalk. So if a teen was so juiced by the booktalk and just had to have the book, he or she had to travel to the library to obtain it. I offered to put them on reserve for them to make it easier to pick up, but I found out that many teens did not have a library card or that the card was blocked by the circulation department for too many fines. In a large system, it is a time-consuming effort to try to match name and address of a teen who did not know or have his or her library card handy. If they had their card, it was easy to jot down the numbers and place a reserve on the title when returning to the public library. The teens still had to come to the library to pick up the book.

Truly great customer service would allow the teens to have instant access to the booktalked books on the spot. However, in my experience there were always circumstances and policies I could not control that prevented this from happening. My best suggestion is to have the printed list of the titles you booktalk available for co-workers back at the public library, so if a teen enters the building, library employees will know what book they are requesting.

Young adult librarians realize it is often necessary to become proactive and meet the teens on their own turf, that is, to enter the school building. When booktalking at a school, make sure you make at least an attempt of suggesting teen books for guys. It is of utmost importance to know the age and reading level of your audience. The audience will probably be mixed, so present books with both girl and boy appeal. Guys tolerate listening to a presentation of romance and character-driven books if they know that some action-packed stories are just around the corner.

RELUCTANT READERS AT SCHOOL

The purpose of attending school is to receive a basic education; and afterwards, a diploma is awarded with satisfactory completion of lessons and tests. Schools have developed detailed instructional lessons in math, science, history, English, foreign language, physical education, and so forth. These lessons are intended to prepare students for the post-high school world. Throughout the curriculum, students are encouraged to read their lessons, take tests, and pass.

Once children have learned the basics of how to read, there seems to be very little attention placed on actual reading skills, other than using this skill as a tool to pass tests. Seemingly, the only time where actual reading instruction takes place is when students are labeled as poor readers, which prompts intervention and remedial reading classes. Of course, this is not how it happens in every school, but it is common enough to warrant some attention.

The point is this: in school, very few students are encouraged to read for pleasure. In school, reading becomes a chore, an act of drudgery that turns students off from reading. This turnoff is especially evident in boys' attitude toward school and reading. In many publications, professionals cite research revealing that the vast majority of young adult reluctant readers are male.

For the majority of people, their first, and probably most consistent, exposure to books, literature, and reading comes through their school experience. And for many teens, the traditional structure surrounding reading works fine. However, for reluctant readers, this same approach may fail. And with male young adult reluctant readers, exposure to books in school may actually turn boys away from reading.

All but a handful of teens learn how to read, but many choose not to take part in any reading experience. Despite their best intentions, teachers and schools (and usually English classes where reading is emphasized), play a big part in developing reluctant teen readers.

HOW SCHOOLS TURN GUYS AWAY FROM READING

One of the more poignant statements I have ever heard about teen reading came from an excellent school librarian, lamenting how teachers in her school continually take a great young adult fiction title, and teach it over and over, until the students could care less. My friend sighed and said, "Once more, school kills book." Schools approach reading as a task to learn concepts about literature and language. Teen boys often do not care to dissect a book; and enthusiasm about reading may be stifled by this approach. In many cases, schools work against themselves by their approach to reading.

English Classes: Overanalyzing the Book

A class read is a good way for teens to share their opinions about the book. In fact, this is one of the benchmark ways to determine whether a book successfully attracts reluctant readers; do they share the book with friends? However, I have witnessed a ninth-grade class spending 9 weeks reading and studying a single book. That title was dissected to the point where the students simply wanted to get rid of the book.

Sometimes a book catches a teen's attention and they read it with a certain level of interest. The teacher then pauses in the middle of the flow of the story and ask students to discuss "why" a certain passage happened. Most boys crave action and a fast-paced story, they do not want to stop and ponder on why something has happened in the book; they want to read quickly to find the next cool thing. In William Golding's *The Lord of the Flies* (a title that has been used in English classes for over 30 years), the character Piggy meets a gruesome death before the story ends. Boys do not want to stop and study the implications of this death; they want to find out if anyone else is going to die and how they will be killed.

English Classes Tend to Exclude Nonfiction from the Curriculum

Nonfiction books, which appeal to many boys, are usually excluded from English class readings. Librarians Jamie Watson and Jennifer Stencel provide a hint for why nonfiction is not used in school settings. In their article, *Reaching Reluctant Readers with Nonfiction*, they state, "Nonfiction continues to be popular with a male audience. But finding the right nonfiction titles for your library collection can be a challenge of its own. Even the most popular titles are rarely reviewed by traditional library journals" (Watson 2005).

In addition to selection issues, there is an underlying prejudice from educators and librarians about nonfiction. In his book, *Reaching Reluctant Young Adult Readers*, author Edward T. Sullivan includes this statement. "One of the most prevalent misconceptions about the role of nonfiction in the lives of young teens is that they read nonfiction just to aid them in homework assignments" (Sullivan 2002).

Biographies are seemingly the type of nonfiction book most likely to be assigned as school required reading. However, *Anne Frank: The Diary of a Young Girl* may not be the best choice for male reluctant readers. In contrast, a biography that seems to appeal to a wide range of males and is now being read in some schools is *Finding Fish* (Fisher, Antwone Q. New York: Morrow, 2001).

Advanced Classes Can Overload on the Classics

In a group setting, any mention of the value and the place of classic literature in teens' literary progression may erupt into a heated debate. Defenses of both sides of the issue can be instantly argued. A certain number of book people insist on a firm foundation of reading based on the classic books. Other book people feel the classics are not essential reading and should not be forced onto the students. This is not the place to discuss the value of the classics, but I suggest that restricting reading to only classical literature will turn off reluctant readers.

I have seen course outlines for advanced senior English classes that require less than 10 books with none of the titles published less than

45 years ago. To exclude contemporary young adult books only alienates the teens; and the teacher then faces an uphill battle to drum up students' enthusiasm for reading. In many high schools, to have the teens buy into their charge, marching bands often incorporate more recent rock songs in their halftime performances while mixing in the oldies. I recall a marching band from a victorious high school playing Chumbawamba's *I Get Knocked Down* after the game ended. (True, the song is from 1998, but the point remains.) If bands can add fresh music to a school function, why should English teachers insist on only presenting classic literature (titles of which may often be over a 100 years old) at the risk of dampening or destroying any student's lifelong interest in reading?

Truly Guy-Friendly Topics Are Often Excluded

Some of the best teachers and librarians do a wonderful job of accepting pop culture into their classes and libraries. They free up time for teens to read and write about what hip-hop poetry means to them, or review the latest movie, or incorporate the latest reality television show into the classroom. Even social satire cartoons such as *The Simpsons* or *Family Guy* may find a spot on the first page of handouts, thus focusing the students' eyes to that page.

But what of guy-friendly topics such as sports, skateboarding, muscle cars, or tattoos? I have had library friends gaze at me with complete blank stares when I mention sports terminology such as low post, tomahawk jam, going yard, bull rushing the quarterback, or freezing the defender with a wicked crossover move. Sports are huge in this country and I have seen guys, wearing gear with team logos plastered all over them, in morning homerooms leaning over the sports page and furiously reading. If the adults who promote reading cannot understand, or do not care to understand, the world of sports, or count reading about sports as real reading; the boys pick up on that and in turn, won't be so receptive to the reading that has been assigned.

Many guys approach me at our library's help desk and exclaim that they are only interested in sports, and they want a sports book. That is the extent of the readers' advisory interview, and I am easily able to direct them to some titles. If you find yourself in the same situation and have no "go-to" title, then your male teen patron will quickly withdraw. Directing the teen male patron to some of the outstanding fiction and nonfiction titles mentioned in previous chapters is a good start to connecting with teen males.

The same thing can be said for anything dealing with automotive repair. Many book people fail to realize that some guys love to talk about 5-speed transmissions, air shocks, and chrome rims.

The point is, there are topics that appeal to both females and males such as movies and music. However, if you really want to find reading material for male reluctant readers—and to have them coming back for more—you need to understand sports and cars.

The Fear Factor

Often many of the titles suggested for reluctant teen readers, in particular reluctant teen male readers, have content on the rough side, by either being very violent or very sexual. Librarians and teachers alike are rightfully concerned about potential backlash from their communities in regard to particular types of books not being appropriate for the audience. In addition to outside official challenges of books from patrons or parents, librarians have been confronted with informal challenges from administrators and co-workers. Often these challenges evolve around a book or magazine that has high appeal to teen male readers. The challenges may be based on language used in the book, sexual or violent content, or even an advertisement with a barely clothed female (or male or both) model in a magazine. If standing alone without the support of a written policy on file with the administration, you have few options. What happens is a disguised type of censorship, under which the titles are simply not purchased and never made available to the patrons. This is exactly what occurred with the publication of Paul Ruditis' 2005 novel, *Rainbow Party* (Ruditis, Paul. New York: Simon Pulse, 2005). Many libraries did not purchase it because in their reasoning, the book was not of high literary value. My simple advice is to be sure that there is a formal written challenge policy on file, and that you, as a librarian, do not fight the good fight by yourself. To undertake an outside challenge alone is most probably a no-win situation for you, your community, and the patrons.

Reading in the Content Area

Recently I gave a presentation about the impact young adult literature has on teens, and how the teen books mirror what often is included in the daily newspaper headlines. Several of the audience members, all secondary school teachers, asked me for suggestions on titles to include in various content areas. They have been charged with including reading across the curriculum and are somewhat desperate for titles in such subjects like math, science, and special education.

When I suggested there were several nonfiction titles about skateboard ramp design, roller coaster loops, and the dimensions of warships, tanks, and submarines, which include math skills, I received shakes of their heads. They had been instructed only to use fiction books. Nonfiction titles, designed to be read for pleasure and great hooks to bring in guy readers, are again often excluded from the curriculum. While there are several recent fiction titles dealing with genetics that can be linked to a science class (Nancy Werlin's *Double Helix* and Margaret Peterson Haddix's *Double Identity* come to mind), I was at a loss to suggest young adult fiction titles that deal with math. I fear because I was not able to immediately suggest fiction titles to them that these math teachers will simply ignore incorporating reading in their curriculum. Once again, reluctant teen male readers lose, as no real effort can be made to include their preferred reading material into the studies.

Although schools have a strong influence on the students' reading, titles suggested by schools do not always come across as something interesting to teen males. Perhaps the school library fiction collection is imbalanced by containing hundreds of titles with girl appeal with only a couple of dozen titles that attract male readers. Perhaps the focus on the library is on curriculum support research rather than pleasure reading. If the collection's only purpose is to enhance the lessons presented in the classrooms, teen males will shy away from using the library's resources. This is not to say that schools are the cause of many boys being reluctant readers, but most reading in school is assigned and teens have no choice but to read what is laid out for them. Schools can provide many strategies to engage teen males into reading and there are schools that provide a valuable service by encouraging guys to simply pick up a book and read.

SCHOOLS CAN INTEREST BOYS IN READING

Schools can play an important role in taking teen males from reluctant reader status to become more avid readers. Recognizing that all students may not be interested in character development of the emotional trauma presented in a story is the first step in engaging reluctant readers. In his essay, *A Defense of Rubbish,* author Peter Dickinson states, "I have always believed that children ought to be allowed to read a certain amount of rubbish. Sometimes quite a high proportion of their reading matter can be healthfully consisting of things no sane adult would actually encourage them to read." Dickinson explains further, "By rubbish I mean all forms of reading matter which contain to the adult eye no visible value, either aesthetic or educational" (Writers, Critics, and Children, 1976).

Reading because you want to is what Stephen Krashen defines as a basis for free voluntary reading (FVR). In his book *The Power of Reading*, he informs us that schools seemingly do not support this type of reading because the benefits are not immediately apparent from testing. Teens are not encouraged, or sometimes even allowed to read for the fun of it. There always seems to be questions at the end of each chapter, or characters to be analyzed. As a teen reader, if you don't care for a book, you must still complete the task or fail. This is probably the only segment of our population that is treated this way. Adult readers give up on books all the time. Professional reviewers tell their audience not to purchase or read a title the reviewer does not like. In school, teens do not have a choice; their grade depends on trying to read what in their opinion is an unreadable book.

Educators who look beyond only providing, or allowing, what they want teens to read have a better chance of developing lifelong readers. Even passively encouraging teens to include in their reading choices items that have no place in the curriculum can create a more enthusiastic teen reader. What follows are some suggestions of ways schools can assist reluctant readers.

Accelerated Reader

Accelerated Reader comes with mixed reviews. Although not all schools participate in this program, the vast majority of schools in the communities where I have worked as a public librarian did (and still do) subscribe to the service.

Upon logging onto the Web page, http://www.renlearn.com, we are told Accelerated Reader will "Build a Lifelong Love of Reading and Learning." Maybe so. However, many professionals lament the fact that Accelerated Reader turns reading into a task or chore and actually discourages students to read. Librarians have conveyed their frustration about how teens only choose Accelerated Reader books and do not want to waste their time reading books that will not award points. Some public librarians passively encourage Accelerated Reader by labeling the books with an identifying sticker and putting the point value on the book.

On the other hand, several librarians admit they push Accelerated Reader titles because the students simply will not read anything else other than books with point values. Whatever your personal opinion, keep in mind that Accelerated Reader is a stepping stone to reading. Whether it creates lifelong readers only time will tell, but it places books in students' hands.

Sustained Silent Reading

In his article, "A Skill for Life" that appeared in *Educational Leadership*, Steve Gardiner states that educators "... often ignore the fact that human beings most frequently succeed at activities they enjoy. We don't need to spend a lot of money or design complicated programs to help students learn to enjoy reading; we just need to give them time to learn that reading can be enjoyable" (Gardiner, *Educational Leadership*, October 2005).

This is one of the most consistently cited ways to transfer reluctant readers into avid readers; to make reading enjoyable. Constantly placing testing as an end result to reading simply turns off teens—they eventually view reading a book as a chore to endure and long to get it over with. Provide teens with time to read what they want and give them a forum to discuss what they are reading with their peers—it is time well spent. Sustained Silent Reading (which is also labeled by a variety of other terms) allows teens the simple freedom to read what they want to read, and quit reading a book if they choose to do so. That is a huge difference from being tested on a make-or-break grade following an assigned reading. Think of it! A teen stops reading and there is no penalty or finger wagging about the downfall of the culture.

Include Audiobooks

Or perhaps we should say, "allow audiobooks." A good narrator can bring a title to life and totally engage the listener. If a reluctant reader has difficulty pronouncing words, following dialogue, or understanding a plot, then audiobooks are a reasonable alternative to actually reading the book. Unfortunately, few educators allow audiobooks to be used in classes. Educators seem to think that listening to a narrator read a book is a form of cheating. Interesting. Although many schools encourage or turn a blind eye to the use of study aids such as CliffsNotes, they do not allow audiobooks, which build valuable listening skills. However, it must be said that while there are benefits in including audiobooks in a school, they are also much more expensive than a paperback edition of the same title. The lack of money may make this option impractical for both school and public libraries.

Introduce Short Stories

Many students fall into the reluctant reader category simply because they don't have, or are unwilling to give up, time to read. By insisting that teens read lengthy novels, you may be sending many students straight to the CliffsNotes section of a nearby bookstore. A short story can delineate a character, introduce and resolve a conflict, and build a suspenseful storyline in less than 20 pages. What's not to like if you are a busy teen with limited time to study?

Come to an Understanding of Graphic Novels and Teen Magazines

The graphic novel is here to stay. For any genre, there is a graphic novel—from adventure and historical fiction to fantasy, science fiction, mystery, romance, and horror. As our world becomes more and more visual, the graphic novel just might be the format that overtakes the print novel as the preferred reading format.

I have presented booktalks to classes where the teacher is a strong advocate for reading, and up-to-date on the latest titles. This same teacher totally opposes graphic novels, and just cannot bring herself to accept them as having any reading value.

The same can be said about magazines. Educators view them as being too easy to read with no real plot or informational value. However, if these items are in the format that attracts teens to reading, let's recognize the power they have. In my library, a recent review of monthly statistics showed that graphic novels had more—about four times more—circulations than regular novels. And many graphic novel readers refuse to read a regular novel even for pleasure.

Budget Cuts? Encourage Small Lending Libraries in Classrooms

If the book budget is slashed, school librarians batten down the hatches and spend money only on items that they feel are absolutely necessary. Often the first items to be eliminated are fiction titles or nonfiction titles that have no direct bearing on the subjects being taught in the classrooms. An alternative solution, where educators can still provide current popular fiction titles is for teachers to include a small personal library in their classes. Teachers have been known to scour public library book sales, petition for grant dollars, and donate their own books to form a small collection in the corner of their classrooms. Some teachers are very nervous about providing these books because they are not familiar with the titles and worry parents will question how the student obtained a title that may have controversial content. Several teachers I know do create access to these edgier books by having a special shelf in their classrooms; the students know this is the place to get the "cool" books. Often these students are reluctant readers who do not visit either the school or public library. Perhaps it is the one-on-one contact with a trusted adult, but teenage boys seem to be less uncomfortable with the informal "checkout" system of a teacher's personal collection.

Create Unique Ways to Evaluate Reading

Schools are under mandates to measure and evaluate all things taught. But does an evaluation on a reading assignment have to be a multiple choice or fill-in-the-blank test? Many teachers who deal with at-risk students, who almost always fall into the ranks of reluctant readers, rarely assign written tests. Instead, they use many creative ways to evaluate if the student read the book. A Readers' Theater scriptwriting and performance is a possible alternative. Writing a poem offering advice to the main character how to deal with his or her conflict is a great way to place a teen "inside the story." I have witnessed teen guys enthusiastically filling out fake death certificates profiling characters that die in the story. With the widespread use of desktop publishing, teens can apply their creativity by making a mock-up of a news story that may include clip art or cut-and-pasted images from the Internet. All these methods engage the reluctant reader more than a standard written test, which may just as easily bore the student.

Of course, a public library is different from a school library. The missions are very different and they play under different sets of rules. In theory, a public library should be more welcoming to teens, especially reluctant readers, than a school library. In theory, the public library should offer types of materials either by format or content that the teens cannot obtain through the school library. However, this is not always the case.

HOW PUBLIC LIBRARIES HURT RELUCTANT READERS

A young adult librarian working in a public library has the unique opportunity to serve teens in a nonthreatening way. For many teens, any adult authority figure in their world immediately presents a negative to them. Schools teachers and administrators must be called Mr. or Mrs. The same schools may have security guards patrolling the hallways and demand from teens the nature of their business. Most small retail businesses discourage teens from entering stores in groups of more than two or three. However, the young adult librarian is someone who can use his or her position to offer help—locate sources for homework, show how to print a document from a computer, or suggest a great book to read. These services can even be accompanied by the suggestion that the teens call him or her by first name. This is the ideal. Unfortunately, public libraries sometimes do things that alienate teens and discourage reluctant readers from even entering the building.

Limited Budgets and Less than Full Teen Service

This still remains a big problem in the library world. While many libraries are on record as having a teen librarian, often this is a split job. Even if it is not a split job, the teen librarian must meet the unwritten expectation to fill in as needed in the running of the library. When budgets for materials are cut, a similar situation to the school library occurs. The library purchases only what they feel is essential and often these items are not what attracts reluctant readers to the public library. The emphasis reverts back to homework help, and research, not pleasure reading. This is especially true of items that are deemed ephemeral, such as magazines and graphic novels.

Lack of Focus for Nonfiction

Nonfiction often does not have any solid presence in a public library's young adult area. In some instances, there is not enough room to include a large number of nonfiction books. In other cases, the library philosophy is to let the adult budget purchase nonfiction and the teens can simply go to that part of the library to obtain the titles they need. Thus reluctant readers cannot easily locate the type of very visual books that attract them. Adult nonfiction is not the same animal as teen nonfiction, and unfortunately teens are forced to use adult titles to fulfill their nonfiction needs. This thinking is a drawback to promoting nonfiction as something that is readable and attractive to male reluctant readers.

Uncertainty about Audiobooks

Many libraries are developing excellent collections of audiobooks. The top titles are often available in both print and audio format. However, some libraries have not created a budget in teen accounts for audiobooks, and purchasing must be done through the adult services or through the audiovisual department. In either case, the selectors do not have contact with teens, and probably are not aware of what titles are needed by teens. The lack of key books available in this format (such as movies adapted from novels) is a missed opportunity with reluctant readers.

Libraries seem to have trouble defining a set policy on selection of audiobooks. They are expensive, much more so than a hardback or paperback edition of the title. There is a constant debate about phasing out cassette tapes and switching entirely over to only audiobooks in CD formats. The technology is constantly changing. Digital versions of audiobooks are coming on to the market that require no cassette or CD, but are self-contained in one battery-operated package. The company Playaway (http://www.playawaydigital.com) is introducing this product to the market and seems to be targeting the teen audience. Other patrons prefer to download audiobooks from their own computer. The wide range of formats and patron preferences automatically makes audiobooks a very expensive endeavor for most libraries. With teen budgets usually being small, purchase of audiobooks for teens takes careful consideration before rushing to randomly select titles.

Lack of Promotion of Reluctant Reader Titles

If the library only staffs teen services with a single person in a split job, then that worker will probably not become familiar with the wide array of materials that might attract a reluctant reader. Displays might only feature award-winning titles, or the librarians' personal favorites. Postings on a Web page may fall under the same criteria, since the quick fix for the harried librarian is simply posting the award-winning titles on the Web page, or perhaps creating a link to recommended reading. Often these titles do not have a high level of attraction to reluctant readers.

Great covers attract reluctant readers and should be displayed face out. But what makes a great cover for teens may be something that bothers adult patrons, especially if the teen area is an extension of the children's area. Some librarians simply choose to avoid the potential problem by not displaying any book with an edgy cover.

Collection Development

Today many libraries emphasize programming as a means to get teens to enter the building. This means something has to give and often what falls to the wayside is the time necessary to produce a quality teen collection that meets all teen needs. With little time, the teen librarian may only order items with starred reviews from their journal. Or, perhaps it is easier to order large numbers of nonfiction curriculum-oriented titles rather than find individual books that will draw a reluctant reader's eyes to its cover. Collection development requires that you create a teen collection to serve the entire population, not just to get books on the shelves by spending the budget quickly. Sadly, books that interest teen male reluctant readers are often the titles that do not get ordered.

HOW PUBLIC LIBRARIES HELP RELUCTANT READERS

While some libraries do not provide ideal services for reluctant readers, other libraries do a wonderful job of drawing into the library teens who do not like to read. What follows are some ways that public libraries can reach out to encourage reluctant readers to visit the public library.

Accelerated Reader

Yes, the same service that may alienate reluctant readers may also provide benefits for them. Many smaller libraries that only serve one school obtain the Accelerated Reader list, make sure the titles are on the shelves, and make it easier for teens searching for these titles to find them. The books are labeled, point values are placed on the cover, and they may even be shelved separately. This is a service that makes it easy for a teen who reads "nothing else" to leave the public library with a title he wants without feeling lost or foolish. Making it hard for a teen to find the Accelerated Reader book he or she wants may discourage reluctant readers from ever returning to the library. Larger libraries serving a wide range of schools find it maddening to attempt to obtain, organize, and label all the different Accelerated Reader titles the various school place on lists, but it's worth the effort.

A Strong Connection to the School

In today's world of slashed materials budgets, not many libraries can include all the great books and materials available for teens. By making a connection with the schools, the teen librarian may be given a heads-up on the next big assignment or when to expect the after-school crowd to demand books on a particular topic. The ability to place the right book into the hands of a reluctant reader helps you gain the trust of the teen. One of the ways you can make reluctant readers feel welcome is to understand the scope and focus of their homework assignments. It is also important not to judge the reluctant reader if he or she tells the librarian that the assignment is due the next day and he or she needs stuff right now! All it takes is a negative facial expression, a clucking of the tongue for a teen who was not that thrilled to enter the library to leave and never return.

Graphic Novel Collections are Booming

Many public libraries have no problems including graphic novels in their teen areas. The main complaint seems to be that they do not have enough money to purchase everything that teens request. Graphic novel collections do not have to follow the established rules of shelving hardback books. The cover artwork is stunning, and it is a disservice to shelve them only by spine out. Face out display is practically a must, so librarians are getting creative in this task. Baskets, old wire racks, and creative placement maybe near computers are all ways to highlight them in a way they can be seen by just a casual glance.

Magazines are Not Just Research Tools

Online databases that provide full text retrieval of periodical articles make storing large amounts of print magazines something of the past. Of course, many libraries, for their own reasons, continue to archive print issues of many titles. However, the need for magazines used by teens for report sources is a fading concept. Teen areas today often display (face out) dazzling magazine covers, there for the simple purpose of pleasure reading. In addition to the availability of news magazines such as *Time* and *Newsweek*, teen areas should include *NewType*, *Fangoria*, *Shonen Jump*, *ESPN the Magazine*, and *GamePro*. These are reading materials that teen guys read and ask for when the next issue is out.

An Overall Positive Atmosphere

As adults frequently present a negative vibe to teen guys in the course of a teen's day, the public library is an institution that can offer something of an oasis to reluctant readers and teen males. Regardless of the reason the reluctant readers have entered the library, a quick glance should allow them to find something that appeals to their interests. It may be a display of skateboarding books, photo essays of professional sporting events, or glossy magazines or graphic novels with enticing cover art. Perhaps it is the high-speed Internet connection that they do not have at home. Teen males who are reluctant readers often wander into a library, and an attractive teen area that promotes appealing reading materials will have these guys returning for more.

Of course, ground rules have to be set so these teens do not disrupt the overall atmosphere of the library. However, these rules should not be so detailed and so prohibitive that the teens have no chance of obeying them, or the staff has no practical way to implement them.

When attempting connections with teens in the twenty-first century, remember that teens may not be in tune with traditional library outreach services. This is a generation that has always known the Internet and are very adept at absorbing any new technology.

Nationwide, librarians are beginning to consider establishing MySpace accounts for their teen services. Library blogs have become somewhat commonplace, and many librarians admirably keep in step with today's teens. But there must be some words of caution before plunging into and embracing electronic technology to connect with teens.

Although it is a great way to engage teens and notify them of the library services, anyone under the age of 18 is still considered a minor. This classification comes with rules. Before blindly creating a MySpace account and inviting your teens to join up, ask your administration about any possible legal hurdles that the technology presents. You might find out that the law is seemingly suspicious of electronically connecting anything with the library and teens. Much like permission forms need to be filled out and signed by guardians to promote a photograph of a teen, a similar document might be required by your library to establish an audio podcast on the library's Web page. The hoops to jump through to establish an electronic presence can be very frustrating. You need to make your decisions if the effort is worth the result. One way to do that is to simply ask the teens if they would like to work with the library to establish an online presence.

The administration's potential hesitation should not deter you from working with teens about establishing an online connection. Most libraries have a Web page, but not all have a teen Web page. If your library does not have one, perhaps now is the time to enlist teens, and guys are very interested in this, about what a teen Web page should contain and what the overall appearance should be. As my library's Web page was constructed by our automation department, we took time to show teens the demo model and asked their opinions. Their advice was insightful and many suggestions came forth that we as adults did not consider. One insightful comment was made when a teen said he understood that a link to homework help should be included on the Web page. His advice was to not put it so prominent near the top of the page. He told us, "The last thing I want to see right away in a Web page is more school stuff."

My library system is in the planning stage of forming a "Teen Tech Advisory Board" where the teens will have input of the content of the teen Web page. It is yet to be determined if they can actually manually change and update the Web page, but we are certainly pursuing gathering their knowledge about the Internet and incorporating their advice to keep the Web page fresh. The initial contacts for this tech advice? They have been almost 90 percent male. Technology is a definite guy magnet.

Librarians working in the constantly changing world of teen services are always searching for ways to enhance service to its audience, especially teen males. Remember, boys are in the schools and building a strong connection with schools in your service area can really produce benefits. Cooperation is the key and it may take some time to build trust between the two institutions. To ignore them, or to neglect to meet them on their own turf, may potentially alienate them and turn them away from the library for good. But do not limit yourself to just schools. Explore other ways to meet guys on their turf, or to offer them opportunities to become involved in what the library has to offer.

REFERENCES

Gardiner, Steve. "A Skill for Life." *Educational Leadership* 63(2) (October 2005), 67–70.

Sullivan, Edward T. *Reaching Reluctant Young Adult Readers.* Lanham, MD: Scarecrow Press, 2002.

Watson, Jamie and Jennifer Stencel. "Reaching Reluctant Readers with Nonfiction." *YALS* (Fall, 2005): 8.

Writers, Critics, and Children. New York: Agathon Press, 1976.

FURTHER READING

Gillespie, John T. and Naden, Corinne J. *Teenplots: A Booktalk Guide to Use with Readers Ages 12–18*. Westport, CT: Libraries Unlimited, 2003.

Krashen, Stephen D. *The Power of Reading*, 2nd ed. Westport, CT: Libraries Unlimited, 2004.

Langemack, Chapple. *Booktalker's Bible: How to Talk about the Books You Love to Any Audience*. Westport, CT: Libraries Unlimited, 2003.

Littlejohn, Carol and Cathlyn Thomas. *Keep Talking That Book: Booktalks to Promote Reading, Grades 2–12*, vol. III. Worthington, OH: Linworth, 2001.

Schall, Lucy. *Booktalks Plus: Motivating Teens to Read*. Englewood, CO: Libraries Unlimited, 2001.

"School Experiments with Same-Sex Reading Groups." *Curriculum Review* (April, 2005): 8.

"Single-Sex Schools Help Close Economic Gap." *USA Today* (May 20, 2002), 11a.

Tyre, Peg. "Boy Brains, Girl Brains." *Newsweek* (September 19, 2005): 59.

———. "The Trouble with Boys." *Newsweek* (January 30, 2006): 44–52.

SUGGESTED WEB SITES

http://www.darwinawards.com. The Darwin Awards.

http://www.nancykeane.com/booktalks. Booktalks—Quick and Simple.

http://www.randomhouse.com/teachers/librarians/booktalks.html. Librarians at Random.

http://www.SingleSexSchools.org.

Chapter 8

ACTIVELY AND PASSIVELY CREATING LIBRARY SERVICES FOR TEEN MALES

Up to this point, the emphasis of this guide has been on how you (who may likely be a one-person show) can be proactive inside and outside the library to create a balance for services for both teen females and males.

This chapter focuses on the teens in the library building. Three aspects of library services to teens, and how you can improve them to better connect with teen males, are discussed. We first focus on the teen area itself and how to make it guy-friendly. The second section in this chapter discusses how libraries can better serve teen males with homework needs. Third, suggestions are offered for other thematic displays that draw boys to the library and the teen area.

Do not feel you must do everything yourself when it comes to providing services to teen males, or, for that matter to the entire teen population. To tackle such a task or believing that the entire tone of services must be generated by one individual leads to two problems. First, stagnation occurs due to a bottleneck, with tasks lined up waiting to be reviewed or accomplished by the teen librarian. Second, this role quickly becomes overwhelming and leads to burn out. Instead of taking everything on yourself, evaluate what you can accomplish within the confines of your budget and your other assigned duties. You'll be providing better service to teens when projects are accomplished in a timely manner, rather than having many "visions" pile up to be simply left hanging, half done, or done poorly.

The pileup of unfinished projects, or those finished haphazardly is essentially what frustrates employees in a department where the supervisor micromanages all aspects of duties and creativity is compressed to minimum efforts or not encouraged at all. If you're a one-person show, how can you avoid falling into the trap of micromanaging yourself? How can you avoid the frustration of not completing set goals and becoming disillusioned? My best advice is to find some things you can manage and accomplish, which promote library services to teen males, and which will be in place over a long period of time. One area that you may be able to control is the teen space in the library.

THE TEEN AREA—WHAT IS IT, WHERE IS IT, AND WHAT DOES IT LOOK LIKE?

Well okay, maybe not total control. Teen areas can be formed and improved by renovating an existing area in the library or adapting a current space dedicated to teens. A teen area can also be made from scratch. By that I mean form a plan from the ground up, incorporating the library administration to be involved with floor plans, acquiring funding, and evaluating a plan for the different types of materials to be made available to teens. I have been involved in both renovation and from-the-ground-up situations, and there are benefits and drawbacks involved with both.

To renovate an existing area is an attractive approach because it usually costs less money than forming a new teen area. If you have a dedicated room that has already been established as a pseudoteen area, then teens are already familiar with the location. The brunt of your work is to make the teen area appear friendly, welcoming, and current; which also involves weeding out unused books and materials.

The main challenge with renovating (or carving out a teen area) is space limitation. Be ready to compromise. Keep that in mind, and know that not all the needs of the teens can be met. This may mean that there just isn't enough room or shelf space for graphic novels or readable nonfiction, two types of books that attract teen males. If you're working within a smaller space, chances are that the teen area will not accommodate a wide range of electronic gadgets (which attract boys to the library).

My best advice is to do your homework before attempting to present a case for a teen area renovation or creation to the administration. Many studies about teen spaces are available—check them out. Your first question is: how much space do you need? In their book, *Teens & Libraries Getting It Right*, authors Virginia A. Walter and Elaine Meyers present a chart comparing square footage of a total library to square footage designated as that library's teen area. Their survey included metropolitan libraries, libraries in smaller cities, and rural libraries. The total percentage of square footage for a teen area falls between 1 and 5 percent of each library's total square footage (Walter 2003).

How much space is enough? Ask any teen librarian about their teen space and they almost always will say they want more space or more electronic items. In each issue of *VOYA*, there is a column, "YA Spaces of Your Dreams." This column features exemplary, newly created and renovated teen spaces. One of the sections is titled, "I Still Dream of These Improvements." There the teen librarians featured in that month's column describe further changes they wish for in their teen areas. Comments about needing more space, needing more electronic connections, and needing a different location altogether, are common (*VOYA*, February 2006).

Having a teen space in their library still remains a goal for many teen librarians. It is possible that the energy and "turf war" that may result from your efforts to create teen areas will cause you to lose focus on the teen patrons. Once the area is established, you may be so euphoric about completing the task that you ignore or neglect keeping the teen males in mind while furnishing the space. There are many pitfalls in this endeavor. Here are some I have come across.

Patterning the Teen Space After a School Classroom

Many librarians love to have the traditional library tables situated in a teen area. For some, their sense of order is disrupted if the tables are not in neat rows and in some sort of straight line. Guys view this regimented arrangement as an extension of school. The idea of four chairs to a table and no chairs at the end of the table is just too structured for them. Instead, put the tables in unique areas near windows, perpendicular to the bookshelves or one long edge of the table facing against the wall to create a quiet study area without totally enclosing the table. This results in less room for chairs, but the teens wishing to concentrate can face the wall and not be distracted by other things going on in the teen area.

Avoid Choosing Only Feminine Decorations

Think of the teen area as a cleaned-up version of a dorm room or a teen's bedroom. Things are not in order. Things are not always color coordinated.

A teen area should be slightly jumbled—not messy, but also not in perfect order. Find some quirky furnishings or decorations that might attract guys and make them somewhat accepting of the area. Several years ago, a local artist donated a huge papier-mâché figure of a woman to the library. This figure stood well over 6 feet tall and the Public Relations department insisted it needed to be displayed, so into the YA area it went. This statue became a place to display popular titles. The teens got a kick out of pulling books from the woman's "arms." It was weird, but the teens accepted this quirky thing. It probably would not have worked in any other part of the library.

Another decorating idea that may send the nonverbal signal that the teen area is guy-friendly is displaying sports posters. Not just the common pro athlete! Find out who in the schools in your service area promotes the high school teams. Many schools produce a large poster that lists the team game schedules throughout the school year. Obtain one and display it in the public library teen area. Of course, if your library serves more than one high school, give equal consideration to all the schools. Play up any rivalry by emphasizing the date of the big game.

A collage of guy things pasted into a display board can be a great attraction. Used and scratched CDs, the print inserts of music CDS, torn covers of video games, DVDs, discarded comic books can all be trimmed and glued and incorporated into a design. The edgier the better to catch guys' eyes and make them feel more comfortable in the teen area. When weeding your collection, don't send an assembly line of abused covers and items to the trash can. To borrow a cliché, one's man's trash is another man's treasure.

Colors for Everyone, Not Just the Girls

For walls, floors, and furniture, use bold or neutral colors, not soft pastels. When painting the walls with murals or decorations, use sharp lines, not only flowing curvy types of illustrations. One obstacle I experienced with a teen area occurred when the administration insisted that all of the items in the teen area "match" the carpet. I argued that this would play a part in discouraging males to come to the teen area. Luckily, the matching color concept was not enforced. It is a simple thing often taken for granted, but a major part of any area of the library is the carpet. It takes up as much, if not more, space than the walls. To entice guys to visit and use the teen area, the first thing they touch (with their feet) cannot be totally feminine, or juvenile. I have visited teen areas in public libraries and chain bookstores that use a star and planet pattern design on the carpeting. It suggests a Disney theme and has very limited appeal to guys over 12 years old. If you are fortunate enough to be allowed input into choosing furnishings and decorations, suggest colors and designs to choices that are somewhat neutral and have equal appeal to both girls and boys.

Promotional Items—Include Guy Stuff

Many teen librarians invest money for the ALA READ posters, which show celebrities holding their favorite book. These posters displayed in a teen area can be quite attractive. If possible buy several of them, laminate each poster, and rotate them for display. Be sure to include celebrities who appeal to guys. Some celebrities that project a welcoming image to teen guys are Coolio, Tony Hawk, Shaquille O'Neal, Ice Cube, and Johnny Damon. For the graphic novel fans, there is also a DC Universe poster featuring practically all of the superheroes. I once had a circulation worker approach me, insisting that she only wanted to see the posters of the hot guys like Sean Connery, Orlando Bloom, or Mel Gibson! I failed to see how displaying only those posters could attract teen males to the area.

Wiring the Area—Insist on It

Push for as much electronic wiring in your teen area as possible. Ask for as many computers as you can fit into the area. And, don't limit the wiring to accommodate only today's needs. Plan ahead, so you can expand electronic materials. DVD players with monitors, projection screens, laptops, and any electronic gaming devices are guy magnets. Don't settle for a teen space that turns out to be some tables, some comfortable chairs, and bookshelves. To bring guys into the teen area, electronic incentives are a must.

HOMEWORK SERVICES TO MALE TEENS

With all the efforts by young adult librarians and library administrations to entice teen males to enter the library with collections and programs, often the only time a teen male takes the initiative to enter a public or school library is to accomplish a homework assignment. Male teens, and also female teens, often enter the library the night before an assignment is due. Putting things off until the last minute is something very characteristic of teens in general—especially of guys. They may not have any idea about the time it would take to accomplish their library research, but they know they need your help. In their rushed state, they may phrase their requests in a way that seems demanding or rude.

Before you lose your cool, remember: this can be a great opportunity to perform quality customer service for teen guys; or a chance to totally alienate the teenager from using the library as an information resource. It is a delicate situation, because for many librarians, the first impulse is to chastise the teen for waiting until the last minute. Ideally, the librarian simply responds to the teen's needs—using reference interview techniques to pinpoint exactly what those needs are, finding how much information is actually needed, how much is readily available, and locating resources for the teen.

When dealing with teen males who approach the reference desk for help, a librarian often attempts to engage them in a conversation. This task at first may appear to be difficult. Remember, during their teen years, many guys are growing. They may not be comfortable with their bodies, and they are often extremely self-conscious. Results of this self-image problem may manifest in mumbling, eyes lowered, or shuffling feet. I have witnessed some reference librarians trying to correct posture, pronunciation, or eye contact before they even attempt to uncover what library materials the guy actually needs.

There is no perfectly right or totally wrong way to do a reference interview with teen guys, but here are some considerations to keep in mind if you want to turn the reference interview into something productive for yourself and your teen patron.

Library Materials May Overwhelm Guys

For many guys, budding egos make them feel as if they should control any situation or environment they encounter. If they are infrequent visitors to the library, they may become immediately confused about the sheer number of books on the shelves or to where in the library to seek help. If a guy feels weak or embarrassed, he will often lash out at, or withdraw from, what is causing him to feel that way. This may burst forth as a direct and blunt but vague question to the reference librarian such as, "You got any books on . . . here?"

In their 2004 *Library Journal* article, "Born with the Chip," authors Stephen Abram and Judy Luther point out, "This generation demands respect and finds no need to beg for good service. In general, they are direct communicators, neither rude nor obsequious, just direct" (*Library Journal*, May 1, 2004).

Reference Desk Atmosphere—An Alien Space?

As mentioned previously, the majority of librarians are female. It is quite possible that a male teen has never had even a semicasual conversation with an adult woman other than family members and teachers. To make matters worse, the reference desk may be situated in a way that it puts the female librarian in a place of authority. I have worked at two general types of reference desks. One where the librarian was seated higher than the patron's eye level and the other where the librarian was seated lower than the patron's eye level. In my experience, the guys were much more comfortable looking down rather than looking up at the librarian. Interestingly, almost all of my female co-workers preferred looking down at the patrons. How is your reference desk situation? If there is a help desk placed in the teen area, I suggest that a chair be made available so a guy can sit and be on equal level with the librarian when he poses his question.

Now, evaluate the décor of the reference area. Is it flowery? Are there materials such as bound notebooks for ready reference information that instead of having a solid color are pastel, patterned, or otherwise feminine in appearance? Teen guys pick up on these little things that can increase discomfort and nervousness.

Guys Google at Home

Teen guys are often adept at computer use. In their minds, the family PC or Mac with Internet access is the place to look for the information they need to complete research for a school assignment. Period. A search engine such as Google may have directed them to all the information they think they need. However, some teachers restrict students from using only Internet sources, so teens come to the library to simply fulfill their need for a single book source on the topic. This approach is completely foreign to many librarians. In fact, a search engine often does the exact opposite of what librarians were trained to do. A search engine will provide practically instant access to content on a given topic and places the source of the information as a secondary matter. Librarians over 40 years old probably were trained to collect citations of sources first, then gather up the content. Often the research philosophy of the librarian and teen are in direct conflict. Keep this in mind when working with teens, and explain your methodology without scolding or patronizing.

Databases—Less Is More

Many libraries have invested hundreds of thousands of dollars to provide online research databases to library cardholders. Have you ever observed teen guys—who are all about technology, who love to hook up electronic devices and can dominate online games—becoming confused by the many electronic research sources typically available at a public or school library? Too often a list of databases is simply that, a list. Librarians, in their zeal to provide as much information as possible, often neglect to provide any real self-help instruction for navigating these databases.

Guys accustomed to using search engines want to get the information quickly and not get hung up trying to search a periodical database and only get a citation (which in their minds is much less than what a search engine provides for them), or a reference to a magazine that is very esoteric and simply not available in most nonacademic libraries.

Teens don't really need to use the many databases crowded in one link on a library's main Web page. Push for (if you don't already have one) a teen Web page that has a link to only a selected list of only homework-help databases that are truly helpful. What teens need are the following types of databases:

- A database that provides full text to periodical articles.
- A science source database.
- A biography source database.
- An historical database that will provide timelines.

These few suggestions can easily be linked to a teen Web page that cuts through the confusion. Depending on your association with the local schools, you may wish to expand to other databases that can be used for homework help for specific assignments that reoccur every year. You can then easily come up with a document online or in print that provides hints on how to navigate those few online databases.

TEEN MALES AND HOMEWORK HELP

The concept of serving teen males with homework help probably seems like something that obviously falls in line with achieving quality teen services for all teen patrons. However, teen males have specific needs in this area that are not always adequately addressed. What follows are some basic suggestions of how to make it easier for guys to achieve homework help at your library. Most of these ideas can actually be applied to both teen males and females.

Tutorials for Online Databases

It is amazing how many teens can run dazzling circles around adults online, but when it comes to obtaining a list of magazines, they do not know how to sort. A brief tutorial about combining search terms, using singular instead of plural words or limiting a search by year or periodical titles would solve many of teen research woes. It is difficult to pass on library search lessons. A class visit to the library may bring around 30 students in the group. Not all libraries have a lab setup that can free up 30 computers. What is effective is to construct brief concise examples of using the databases through an Internet connection viewed on a large screen with a LCD projector. Make the searches examples of what can go *wrong* with a sample search (i.e., too broad of a subject search, incorrect spellings or an historical topic not located in a periodical database). Teens are more receptive to seeing potential mistakes than a lengthy, and potentially boring, explanation of the correct way to navigate the database. Include shortcuts to finding information. Teens may surprise you on how much they know about manipulating an electronic source; they just may not know they can apply their Internet surfing skills on a library database.

If you produce a teen newsletter, either in print or online, include a quick bulleted list of tips on how to access the libraries homework help databases. This can be an item that appears in each issue. Teachers will be more apt to distribute the newsletter if they see immediate benefits to their instructions. It does not make sense for a library to invest money to obtain these databases if they are not used. When formulating an instructional package, make sure your information is to the point and concise. Teens, especially teen males, will not read through a 4- to 5-page manual on how to utilize an electronic source.

Access to the Schools

Make a connection with the school media specialist and offer to come to the school to do an instructional period about using the public library's catalog or databases. I have found that several school media centers have an area that is more of a lab setup, where formal instruction can be more effective than trying to accomplish the same task in a public library's teen area. Remember, a strong connection with the school can have benefits. For example, if you connect with teachers, you'll more likely be informed when a major report topic is due, and even be able to secure a list of the topics. Of course, your task may be more daunting. Teachers can be notorious about taking care of their own arena and not changing procedures. They may not have even a base inkling about the sweeping changes computers have brought to the library business.

However, many teachers are simply unaware of what the public has to offer; and some may be totally clueless on what a research database can do. Case in point. I had an eighth-grade boy, about 4 years ago, approach me about gathering information on a report about steroids. He had done his online research through a periodical database and found a citation for an older magazine. He asked if that issue was available in print. I told him no, but explained what full-text meant and showed him how he could see the article, send the text to his e-mail address, review it at home, and print it if needed. The problem? The teacher told the student (I learned the next time I saw the young man) that the information was not valid because it came from a computer and the teacher would not allow any unverified sources from the Internet. The teacher said, "If it came from inside a computer, I won't allow it." This example illustrates the broad differences between two generations of library users. The teachers often need to be educated along with the teens.

Teen Males and Librarians—Let's Talk

As stated earlier in this book, teen males often mumble and may not have the most sophisticated verbal communication skills. This is not going to change with a disapproving look from a librarian. What is needed is an engaging sentence or phrase that enables a teen guy to gain some ownership into the reference interview. Two such phrases that have worked for me are, "Let's see if we can work together to get what you need," and "I need your help before we start." These phrases seem to put the teen and the librarian on a somewhat level playing field before any selection of materials begins. Other statements that help pinpoint the search are, "What class is this for?" and "How much do you need?"

For librarians working in an online after-hours environment, these phrases also are effective to get to the point of what the teen actually needs. Of course there is no positive way to determine if the online patron is a guy or even a teen. Librarians who have worked on homework help sites have expressed their frustration with how the teens seem to be rude and demanding. My guess is that these teens are guys who are frustrated with their lack of power to dominate, as they do in video games and other electronics; and they are pressed to ask for help from a librarian. Even anonymously online, guys may hate appearing to be weak and lash out with direct and blunt comments.

Guy Topics in the Teen Nonfiction Collection

There may be the day that a teacher in your service area follows all the procedures correctly, contacts you, and sets up a tutorial session of how to electronically retrieve information. The problem is this: the teacher may not exactly assign topics to the students, but the assignment is something along the lines of "topic of choice" where the goal is the research process. So naturally, teen males will want to report on things that interest them. The not unrealistic stipulation is that the teacher requires a variety of sources such as an Internet site, a magazine article, and a book source. If you have time and enough of an advance alert, a sound course of action is to formulate a list of topics on which you feel the teens will be able to locate plenty of information. Of course, many nonfiction topics can be utilized by either sex. Commonly asked for topics such as abortion, drug use, teen rights, and crime are report topics both boys and girls choose. But if given a choice, boys usually select topics that are solidly guy-oriented. Be sure to include on your list of suggestions topics such as sports skills training, automobile engine maintenance, weaponry both modern and medieval, special forces training, terrorist tactics, graffiti artwork, hip-hop culture, gang violence, teenage crime and punishment, Web page design, video game design, and computer maintenance and construction. Of course, the budget might have the final say on how many titles can be purchased for the nonfiction section, but the thought is to pay attention to the needs of the teen males. They may want to learn about, or form a report on, topics that mostly appeal to guys.

Homework Help Equals Customer Service

Determining an approach to homework help can be problematic. What is the librarian's role when a teen asks for help in locating materials? Should you point to the general area where materials are shelved? Should your scribble down the Dewey numbers and pass a note to the teen? Or should you physically locate the books, pull them off the shelves, and place them into the teens' hands? If you do this, will you feel like you are doing the work while the teen simply stands there?

Unless there is a lineup at the help desk, I usually escort the teen to the area where they can find the materials they need for the assignment. On the way, I offer a quick library lesson about Dewey numbers, mentioning that like subjects are shelved together. This chat probably won't instantly transform the teen into a self-sufficient patron, but it does plant the seed. This also relaxes the teen (especially teen males) after possibly being nervous from asking his or her initial question. Using this moving reference interview technique you often find that the teen may not need an overwhelming amount of material, but is just looking for the basic information about the topic. Sometimes all they need is a timeline about the event they have been assigned, or the main personalities involved. These facts would be very difficult to find by themselves. The librarian who hands out a Dewey number shelf location will never realize what exactly the teen patron needed.

Are teen guys seeking different types of library help than teen girls? Not really. In my experience the homework assignments are from a random list allowing teens to pick their topic. Nineteenth century authors can be presented in a list, allowing both male and female students pick a name that sounds interesting. It might be a science report about the person who invented a particular item. What stands out about guys and these information-gathering tasks is that they really do not want to endure the process of searching a catalog or database. They are willing to study the material, if it is placed in their hands. In my observations, teen girls are generally more willing to use an index, or jot down possible titles and subject headings and then go get the material. It seems guys want the quickest and easiest route to the information.

Once you are established in your library service area and become aware of recurring assignments, you may wish to construct a file that includes great information on the assignments. A pathfinder sheet that suggests alternative subject headings, places to search, and what is the actual topic of their assignment is a great help to teens. Will information about the London police force in the Victorian era be found in books about Victorian London or in a history of police forces? As librarians, we relish the search process. Teen males abhor it. Any shortcut to finding homework information will be greatly appreciated by teen males. And they will come to view you as someone who knows what they are going through and that you are willing to help. This all translates into solid customer service.

TEEN WEB PAGE

Teens are in tune with the electronic communication from their cell phones to any Internet site such as YouTube and MySpace that connects with other teens. Libraries are plunging into the world of electronic communication, albeit some libraries more slowly than others.

Most libraries have a Web page, but not all have a teen Web page. A Web page is an effective way to communicate with teens without going through hassles of printing a flyer generated by an already overworked graphics department. Anything that can be produced in print (bibliographies, new titles, annotations, opinions about books, and program announcements) can be more quickly posted on a library's teen Web page.

Teen guys are hooked to electronics and love to tinker with gadgetry. Here is an opportunity to either formally, or informally, enlist their interest and apply it to the changing content of your Web page. As a young adult librarian, you may find it difficult to budget time to change the appearance and content of your Web page. However, it must be fluid and changing or it will not appeal to teens.

A long-range plan may be to have a specialized teen advisory board that only works with or evaluates the teen Web page. This is a big draw for guys. It will connect them to the library and allow them to contribute to teen services in a positive way.

Given below are some tips about a teen Web page to make it guy-friendly:

- Don't clutter the Web page with many links that lead to confusion.

- Have a button that takes teens to homework help or research databases. Don't have that be the first thing they see.

- Ask the guys you serve what is cool and interesting. Your idea of a neat Web site might be very old news to them.

- If podcasting or using pictures to promote teen services, have teens produce it. Teens logging onto a Web page's podcast should hear other teens' voices, not a librarian droning on about a topic. They want to see picture of their peers, not employees of the library working at a program. A word of caution: Many libraries require a release form signed by a guardian before allowing a teen's voice or picture to be used on a Web site. It is best to check with all levels of administration before plunging into this project.

- Post content on your Web page that is in some way interactive. Can they add their thoughts to a posting? Can they change content? Teens want to control the Web, not just read what is shown.

- Make colors and fonts edgy and teen-appealing. Use the models of top retail sites that target teens. Chances are those Web pages do not look like the library's main Web page.
- Bold is good. Teen guys want to know if the site is interesting in the first 3 seconds they log onto that page. Thus, the title font is very important.

Your teen Web page can be every bit as effective a method to entice teen guys into your library as a program targeting them. You may find out that some teen guys enjoy being anonymous behind the scenes while building content on a Web page. This is the appeal of a chat room. Indeed, in our live author chats at my library, there are many guys logging on to discuss books and writing. (We can never be completely positive they are guys, as they use pseudonyms in the chat environment.)

The drawback to attracting teen guys to an advisory meeting with technology? The technology is constantly changing and you may quickly find yourself lost in the jargon. Don't panic. This is the time to facilitate what is going on by establishing order and a time frame and simply ask questions about what they would like to see on a library Web page. The guys will respect you more if you ask for their expertise rather than trying to bluff your way through the meeting. Chances are they know more than you when it comes to Web use and design. Technology presents a vehicle to really connect with the guys, use it to your advantage.

DISPLAYS IN THE TEEN AREA

Displays are constructed with two goals in mind, to promote library materials—new and old—and to encourage patrons to browse materials they would not normally select. In both large and small libraries, display areas are a key component to the facility. Cases designated only to display materials are permanent structures in many departments of libraries. Behind sliding glass doors, encased by solid wood walls, the treasures of the library are offered to the viewing public.

Some displays are patterned after museum displays, where unique or rare items are put on view, not intended to circulate away from the building. Many public libraries' local history departments employ this approach with their displays—that they are a "look-but-do-not-touch" arrangement. Often the glass doors are locked, preventing patrons from laying hands on the valuable materials.

On the other hand, many library departments use displays to promote their materials, hoping that patrons on an impulse moment will select an item and take it home. This concept is very similar to how supermarkets and other retail stores merchandise their products. Marketing the library's collection is a science unto itself and beyond the scope of this book. A comprehensive plan to market and display library materials is offered in Mary Anne Nichols' *Merchandising Library Materials to Young Adults* (Greenwood Village, CO: Libraries Unlimited, 2002). In this book, you will find dozens of fresh ideas to enhance your teen area and increase circulation of materials.

If your teen area is a niche in the library that you have struggled to carve out, then chances are you don't have a fabulous display case to show off the teen materials. Some teen librarians have become very clever at creating offbeat methods to display using materials gathered from other departments—cast-off magazine racks, paperback display stands, or small bookcases that were designated for the dumpster. Such is the life of a teen librarian. Often you are expected to make do with little or no new furniture or display fixtures.

But that does not mean that teen materials have no opportunity to be placed on display. It is no secret that teens are visually prompted when it comes to selecting materials. Putting books, magazines, and audiobooks on display utilizing a variety of techniques makes the teens feel that the teen area is more accessible. Use displays to promote different sections of your nonfiction collection, promote new titles, or construct themes that display both fiction and nonfiction titles on a topic. Staying with the focus of this book, this section can include ideas and suggestions for displays that have teen male appeal.

But are there other "outside-the-box" types of creations that use displays to further engage teens, especially teen males, and interest them into using the library? Displays don't always have to lead back to a book, or simply show a book's cover. A dedicated display area is a great way to connect with the schools in the library's service area or perhaps a niche part of the community. Of course, our focus is to create displays that simply catch the eye of the teen male who happens to be browsing through the teen area.

If there are dedicated cases that can be locked, this is a great place to display collections of different items. It surprised me, but I once placed rocks in a case and labeled them as sedimentary, igneous, etc. Guys were fascinated and I cannot explain why. Perhaps they just liked looking at the different colors and shapes. Admittedly, I was lucky to have this collection handy from my own youth; and it included some visually interesting examples of stones smoothed and hollowed out by erosion. I can only say that perhaps the guys got interested because it was not an in-school lecture about the rocks. I wanted to follow-up the rock display with an arrowhead collection, but could not locate one that the owner was willing to lend for display. No matter, the point is this: Sometimes it is not the obvious items that attract the attention of teen males.

To expand on the thinking of displaying objects rather than books, use your connection with the school to display teen artwork. Most schools enter the students' top work into an art show, but there is no reason why other items cannot be displayed in the public library. The great thing about an art display is that it can include drawings, paintings, and sculptures. I definitely advise locking up any object that has the slightest value, even sentimental value.

In a time when I was at a loss for ideas of display items, I decided to incorporate a display into a contest. I simply gathered some weird-looking things that teens may recognize but could not immediately identify by name. I included some antiques like a small washboard, an iron that was not electric, and a wooden spoon with a hole in the middle that was used for carrying hot hard-boiled eggs. Items were numbered and teens could win a small candy bar for even attempting to identify the items. To encourage guys, I included things like spark plugs, an oil dipstick, a football helmet chinstrap, and so on. There was absolutely no true educational objective to the display and there was no connection back to the book, but the teens, especially teen males, were engaged.

Another suggestion for a display may be dicey for you, but I believe it is worth considering. That is science fair projects. I believe it is a must that these are locked up in a "look but do not touch" location. In my experience, science fair has been a huge project for schools in the service area and at other places I have been employed the schools did not sponsor a fair. Check with your school. At times the winning entries may take up a large area with a trifold display board, but to show a winning entry may be a way to connect teens back to the library's collection. Many libraries have extensive files and resources on science fair projects and it only makes sense in these cases to display an outstanding effort by a teen. And often, teen males turn in quality projects.

REFERENCES

Abram, Stephen and Luther, Judy. "Born With the Chip." *Library Journal* (May 1, 2004): 34–37.

Walter, Virginia A. and Meyers, Elaine. *Teens & Libraries Getting It Right*. Chicago, IL: American Library Association, 2003.
"YA Spaces of Your Dreams." *VOYA* (February 2006): 674–675.

FURTHER READING

http://www.alastore.ala.org. Graphics: Celebrity READ.
Braun, Linda W. *Hooking Teens with the Net*. New York: Neal-Schuman, 2003.
Nichols, Mary Anne. *Merchandising Library Materials to Young Adults*. Greenwood Village, CO: Libraries Unlimited, 2002.
Taney, Kimberly Bolan. *Teen Spaces: The Step-by-Step Library Makeover*. Chicago, IL: American Library Association, 2003.

✺ ✺ ✺ ✺

Conclusion

This book is an attempt to increase your awareness of a group of patrons that very well may be underserved in your library—teenaged males. Many young adult librarians are fighting the good fight to improve services to all teens, but you may not have a solid "game plan" on how to provide library services to teen males. The purpose of this book is to help you formulate a game plan that includes this population.

The teenage years are tough for many teens. For teen males, entering a library that may be exclusively operated by an all-female staff may cause the young men to feel uncomfortable, out of place, or confused about how to act. In addition, if you are unsure how to approach the young man or have no real feeling for what makes him tick, then the opportunity for quality service to that one patron has met an immediate brick wall.

Throughout the book, I have tried to provide insight on how guys feel, what interests them, what they like to read, and how their preferences can be incorporated into improving library services to teen males. There is no magic answer or solution to what many librarians view as a problem in their library—that is, how to connect with the teen guys.

Service for all teens must achieve a balance between the components of the library facility, the library collection, and the service attitude of the library staff. These three components must be consistent in providing all library patrons with materials and services for which they have entered the building. If any of the components becomes skewed, the overall service to a patron group may be found lacking. This is the situation that I believe occurs in many libraries in regard to male teens. Hopefully this book has provided you with some suggestions that have provoked your thought to improve services to them.

I have focused on practical suggestions rather than theories about how to provide services for the teen males in the library. If I have made errors, I tried to make them in favor of the teen males.

I have stated repeatedly that guys feel uncomfortable if they are forced into a situation where they view themselves as weak, inferior, or effeminate. This may not be true for all guys or occur on a regular basis in your library, but I am certain it happens often enough for librarians to take note. If this book causes you to reevaluate yourself and your services to guys, and those services show improvement by more teen males entering the library and asking for assistance, then this effort has been a success.

APPENDIX

ESSENTIAL FICTION TITLES OR SERIES FOR TEEN MALES

Although using the term "essential" may open the door to all sorts of arguments, I believe this list offers something for most teen male readers interested in fiction. Several of the titles have been mentioned earlier throughout this book.

Adoff, Jaime. *Jimi & Me.* New York: Jump at the Sun/Hyperion, 2005.
Anderson, M.T. *Feed.* Cambridge, MA: Candlewick Press, 2002.
Black, Jonah. *The Black Book: Diary of a Teenage Stud.*
 Girls, Girls, Girls. New York: Avon, 2001.
 Stop, Don't Stop. New York: Avon, 2001.
 Run, Jonah, Run. New York: Avon, 2001.
 Faster, Faster, Faster. New York: Avon, 2002.
Colfer, Eoin. *Artemis Fowl Series*
 Artemis Fowl. New York: Hyperion, 2001.
 Artemis Fowl: The Arctic Incident. New York: Hyperion, 2002.
 Artemis Fowl: The Eternity Code. New York: Miramax/Hyperion, 2003.
 Artemis Fowl: The Opal Deception. New York: Miramax/Hyperion, 2005.
Cormier, Robert. *After the First Death.* New York: Pantheon, 1979.

Coy, John. *Crackback*. New York: Scholastic, 2005.

Crist-Evans, Craig. *Amaryllis*. Cambridge, MA: Candlewick Press, 2003.

Crutcher, Chris. *Whale Talk*. New York: Greenwillow Books, 2001.

———. *The Sledding Hill*. New York: Greenwillow Books, 2005.

Curtis, Christopher Paul. *The Watsons Go to Birmingham—1963*. New York: Delacorte Press, 1995.

———. *Bucking the Sarge*. New York: Wendy Lamb Books, 2004.

Delaney, Joseph. *Revenge of the Witch: The Last Apprentice: Vol. 1*. New York: Greenwillow, 2005.

de la Pena, Matt. *Ball Don't Lie*. New York: Delacorte Press, 2005.

Draper, Sharon. *Tears of a Tiger*. New York: Antheneum, 1994.

Farmer, Nancy. *House of the Scorpion*. New York: Antheneum, 2002.

Flake, Sharon G. *Bang!* New York: Hyperion, 2005.

Flanagan, John. *The Ruins of Gorlan. Ranger's Apprentice:* New York: Philomel, 2005.

Flinn, Alex. *Breathing Underwater*. New York: HarperTempest, 2002.

Giles, Gail. *Playing in Traffic*. Brookfield, CT: Roaring Brook, 2004.

Hiaasen, Carl. *Hoot*. New York: Alfred A. Knopf, 2002.

———. *Flush*. New York: Alfred A. Knopf, 2005.

Horowitz, Anthony. *Alex Rider Series.*

    Stormbreaker. New York: Puffin Books, 2001.

    Point Blank. New York: Scholastic, 2002.

    Skeleton Key. New York: Philomel, 2003.

    Eagle Strike. New York: Philomel, 2004.

    Scorpia. New York: Philomel, 2005.

    Ark Angel. New York: Philomel, 2006.

Horowitz, Anthony. *Raven's Gate*. New York: Scholastic, 2005.

Hughes, Dean. *Soldier Boys*. New York: Antheneum, 2001.

Jenkins, A. M. *Damage*. New York: HarperCollins, 2001.

———. *Out of Order*. New York: HarperCollins, 2003.

Johnson, Angela. *The First Part Last*. New York: Simon & Schuster, 2003.

Klass, David. *You Don't Know Me*. New York: Frances Foster Books, 2001.

———. *Dark Angel*. New York: Farrar, Straus & Grioux, 2005.

Korman, Gordon. *Son of the Mob*. New York: Hyperion, 2002.

Lubar, David. *Sleeping Freshmen Never Lie*. New York: Dutton, 2005.

Lupica, Mike. *Travel Team*. New York: Philomel, 2004.

MacHale, D. J. *The Pendragon Series*

    The Merchant of Death. New York: Aladdin, 2002.

    The Lost City of Faar. New York: Aladdin, 2003.

    The Never War. New York: Aladdin, 2003.

    The Reality Bug. New York: Aladdin, 2003.

    Black Water. New York: Aladdin, 2004.

    The Rivers of Zadaa. New York: Simon & Schuster, 2005.

Martino, Alfred C. *Pinned*. Orlando, FL: Harcourt, 2005.

McNamee, Graham. *Acceleration*. New York: Wendy Lamb Books, 2003.

Mikaelsen, Ben. *Touching Spirit Bear*. New York: HarperCollins, 2001.

Myers, Walter Dean. *Monster*. New York: HarperCollins, 1999.

Olin, Sean. *Killing Britney*. New York: Simon Pulse, 2005.

Paulsen, Gary. *Hatchet*. New York: Antheneum, 1987.

Paver, Michelle. *Wolf Brother. Chronicles of Ancient Darkness #1*. New York: Harper-Collins, 2004.

Plum-Ucci, Carol. *The Body of Christopher Creed*. San Diego, CA: Harcourt, 2000.

Reeve, Philip. *Mortal Engines*. New York: Scholastic, 2001.

Rollins, James. *Amazonia*. New York: William Morrow, 2002.

———. *Ice Hunt*. New York: William Morrow, 2003.

Rowling, J. K. *The Harry Potter Series*
    Harry Potter and the Sorcerer's Stone. New York: A.A. Levine Books, 1998.
    Harry Potter and the Chamber of Secrets. New York: A.A. Levine Books, 1999.
    Harry Potter and the Prisoner of Azkaban. New York: A.A. Levine, 1999.
    Harry Potter and the Goblet of Fire. New York: A.A. Levine, 2000.
    Harry Potter and the Order of the Phoenix. New York: A.A. Levine, 2003.
    Harry Potter and the Half-Blood Prince. New York: A.A. Levine, 2005.

Sachar, Louis. *Holes*. New York: Farrar, Straus & Giroux, 1998.

Salisbury, Graham. *Eyes of the Emperor*. New York: Wendy Lamb Books, 2005.

Shan, Darren. *The Saga of Darren Shan Series*
    Cirque du Freak. Vol. 1. Boston: Little, Brown, 2001.
    The Vampire's Assistant. Boston: Little, Brown, 2001.
    Tunnels of Blood. Boston: Little, Brown, 2002.
    Vampire Mountain. Boston: Little, Brown, 2002.
    The Vampire Prince. New York: Little, Brown, 2002.
    Trials of Death. New York: Little, Brown, 2003.
    Hunters of the Dusk. New York: Little, Brown, 2004.
    Allies of the Night. New York: Little, Brown, 2004.
    Killers of the Dawn. New York: Little, Brown, 2005.
    The Lake of Souls. New York: Little, Brown, 2005.
    Lord of the Shadows. New York: Little, Brown, 2006.

Shusterman, Neal. *Full Tilt*. New York: Simon & Schuster, 2003.

Sniegoski, Tom. *Sleeper Agenda*. New York: Razorbill, 2006.

Sniegoski, Tom. *Sleeper Code*. New York: Razorbill, 2006.

Tashjian, Janet. *The Gospel According to Larry*. New York: Henry Holt, 2001.

Trueman, Terry. *Stuck in Neutral*. New York: HarperCollins, 2000.

———. *Inside Out*. New York: HarperTempest, 2003.

Volponi, Paul. *Black and White*. New York: Viking, 2005.

Wallace, Rich. *Wrestling Sturbridge*. New York: Alfred A. Knopf, 1996.

———. *Playing without the Ball*. New York: Alfred A. Knopf, 2000.

Westerfeld, Scott. *Midnighters #1: The Secret Hour*. New York: Eos, 2004.

———. *Midnighters #2: Touching Darkness*. New York: Eos, 2004.

Wilson, Diane Lee. *Black Storm Comin'*. New York: Margaret K. McElderry, 2005.

Woodson, Jacqueline. *Miracle's Boys*. New York: G. P. Putnam's Sons

INDEX

About the Author

ROLLIE JAMES WELCH is Teen Coordinator of the Cleveland Public Library System. He has worked as a librarian, mostly with teens, for 26 years in both school and public library settings. A frequent presenter at local library workshops throughout his home state of Ohio, Rollie has served on the YALSA book selection committees, Quick Picks for Reluctant Young Adult Readers, and Best Books for Young Adults. He has also chaired *VOYA*'s Top Shelf for Middle School Fiction committee. He is a reviewer for *Kirkus*, *VOYA*, *Library Journal*, and *The Cleveland Plain Dealer* newspaper.